Under

Producer & International Distributor
eBookPro Publishing
www.ebook-pro.com

Underneath a changing sky
Yaron Reshef

Copyright © 2023 by Yaron Reshef
Another Planet Publishing
Reshef.book@gmail.com
Translation: Nina Rimon Davis
Proofreading: Camilla Conlon
Cover Design: www.ebook-pro.com

Produced by Notssa – www.notssa.com
Library of Congress Control Number: 2020912847

ISBN: 9798376480816

This book is dedicated to the memory of Dr. Syma Finkelman, my aunt, whom I was not fortunate enough to ever meet.

One's recollections of a person ought to be nurtured. That is the only way to preserve them. Nurturing is done through a story that breathes life and validity into them. You relate the memories, and they return the favor by growing stronger and creating a safe, permanent spot in your consciousness, until they become part of you.

Contents

Syma	7
Sailing to Haifa	9
Palestine	45
Second Dream	80
Khayat Beach	95
Ethel	97
Jerusalem	109
6, Nordau	128
Third Dream	136
Letter to Zelda – 21 July, 1935	142
On the Train – 18 November 1942	146
Hope is the Enemy of Fear	152
At the Belzec Station – 19 November, 1942	153
Shaanxi Earthquake, China 1556	161
The Characters in the Story	163
About the Book	164
Belzec Memorial Site, 2013	170
Acknowledgements	172

Syma

When I asked my father about the origin of my name, he replied, "Syma means 'my treasure' in Aramaic", as if he already knew since the day I was born that, one of these days, we'd all be digging in our yards and burying the things we treasured most, until the worst was over. "Your name comes from The Midrash, an interpretation of The Song of Songs: 'and he dug therein and found syma,' he went on to quote from the Talmud, and added: "Rabbi Shapira helped us choose your name; the word "syma" is a good luck charm, bestowing a good life."

My sister Zelda, on the other hand, used to interpret my name based on its numerological value of seven: "People whose name equals seven are serious and introverted, unique personalities who aspire to wholeness and perfection, who are critical and skeptical and do not simply accept things at face value. They examine and investigate everything, and once they reach a conclusion, they take it to its utmost limit. Meaning they can easily turn from skeptics to fanatics." Over time, life was to prove Zelda right. I liked to be alone; I needed my own quiet nook.

My sister Zelda was eight years older than I. She was the 'spiritual' sort while I was the science-oriented one. She loved philosophy and playing the piano, while I dedicated myself to medicine, even though I, too, appreciated philosophy and music.

When it came to love, I was both sensitive and impassioned. But if it led to disappointment I'd cut off all ties coolly and quickly. Thus I often found myself alone.

***

Sailing to Haifa

How strange it was to plan a boat trip to Palestine, or Eretz Israel – the Land of Israel, as we preferred calling it – on a ship called Polonia. This was one of the ships that sailed every other week from Constanta, Romania to Haifa. En route, the ship stopped for several hours in Constantinople, Piraeus, and sometimes in Cyprus, reaching Haifa within a week. They said that sailing was quite safe. "The Mediterranean is calm, it isn't an ocean," said my brother-in-law, Karl, repeating what everyone else was saying. But these words failed to reassure me. Small wonder; only in January a ship ran into a storm and one of its passengers died, the papers reported. "The sea is the sea. And since I have neither gills nor fins, I'm afraid," was my standard retort to everyone.

I started toying with the idea of a trip to Palestine even before Father passed away, but Junio, my younger brother, beat me to it. He was determined to leave Chortkow. He was sick and tired of everything: Mother's nagging; being the only man in a home full of women; the difficulty of finding clients to design and build houses for; and mainly tired of

Menachem Mendel Kramer's refusal to let him marry his daughter, Malca. I guess we weren't kosher enough for these Hassidim, or else perhaps not rich enough, since "architecture isn't a very promising way of making a living." Or maybe the objection came from his wife, Fradel, since she was the one who called the shots. She was the one who managed the Kramers' business, and it was common knowledge that thanks to her their business boomed and they got rich. Indeed, Fradel was a smart woman and a shrewd dealer.

In a brilliant move, Junio secured an immigration certificate for himself. He enrolled for engineering and architecture studies at the Technion in Haifa; then, with his typical creativity, rewrote his curriculum vitae, changing the data of his architecture studies in Vienna to look like high-school studies, and thus he was accepted to the Technion. One morning he got on the train to Constanta and sailed to Palestine.

When Father died, I made the final decision to go away, too. I needed some air, some variety. Mother had been directing all her energies at me, getting involved in every aspect of my life. Since she was no longer able to order my father around, she apparently decided to order me around: "Why do you work till all hours of the night? Why don't you go out more?' And the worst was her pestering me about men – a sensitive issue for a thirty-five year old single woman.

I've always been independent, and the trip to the East did not scare me. I was curious to know what my life in Palestine would be like, should I decide to leave Poland. Truth be told, life in Chortkow was a cosseting existence. I was both spoiled and bored. On the one hand, it was very convenient to live in my family home, just a few steps away from the hospital, and very close to my sister Zelda, her husband Karl, and their two sons, Adam and Zigush. I had my own clinic and regular patients, whose numbers kept growing. On the other hand, I lacked challenges. I'd cut back on my activities in the Shomer HaTzai'r movement, I'd stopped undertaking assignments as accompanying physician for youth groups on various hikes and outings, and I missed the political arguments I used to have with Junio. The latter was a proud Revisionist Zionist, whereas I was skeptical about Zionism. I used to claim that all political activists were the same and that there was no big difference between the various Zionist ideologies – they all reflected current European views rather than any original thought.

With time, my social circle seemed to shrink. Most of my friends got married and, whenever I was invited to an event by a couple of close friends or by a family, I hated being a third wheel, the odd one out. Thankfully, my relationship with Zelda and Karl was different and I always enjoyed spending time with them. Especially with Adam, whom I referred to as a wonder-child; he knew books by heart in both Polish and Latin; everyone foresaw a brilliant future for him.

Given all the above, when I first heard that the first Israeli congress for Jewish physicians was to take place in Tel Aviv on April 23rd, 1936, I immediately decided to attend.

It was quite clear to me that, in the long run, there was no future for us in Poland. The economic situation continued to deteriorate, while anti-Semitism flourished. Admittedly, our situation in Chortkow was relatively good: we were not exposed to the debilitating poverty and plagues rampant in other areas and in the big cities. But the disquiet began bubbling underneath our feet, particularly after the death in May 1935 of Dziadek "Grandpa" – Marshal Jozef Pilsudski, our beloved leader, founder of the Second Republic of Poland.

"Grandpa" was a proponent of the view that Poland is a multi-ethnic state and that we, the Jews, were one of its ethnicities. Which meant the Jews were Polish nationals. Thus I, too, grew up believing in the supremacy of the state over ethnicity. I believe this approach is what enabled life in Chortkow, where the population was comprised of one third Poles, one third Ukrainians, and one third Jews. There was no love lost between these different ethnic groups; or, to be precise, hatred was rampant both between the Ukrainians and the Poles (the Ukrainians felt put-upon because they were ruled by the Poles), and between the latter two and us, the Jews.

On the other side, opposite "Grandpa"'s party, known as the Sanation, was the Nationalist camp. They were horrible towards us; a lethal combination of nationalism and anti-Semitism. They considered us – the three and a half million Jews in Poland – foreigners, and the chief cause of all their troubles. They were simply fascists who wanted to get rid of us by any means available. The leader of the nationalist, anti-Semitic camp was a nasty type, Roman Dmowski, who believed that our mere existence in Poland was a disaster for society. I remember his words clearly: "They are lethal to our society, and we must get rid of them so that Poland does not turn into Judeo-Poland." Like many other anti-Semites, he compared us to "a well-organized swarm of locust that is devouring every good patch of Polish land", and used to add "We've got to show them the door, so as to make Poland free of Jews." I was appalled by the way the Nazi racial theory was attracting enthusiastic Polish supporters. This fascist process was led by the bastards from the Endecja party. They considered the actions of the Nazi German regime to be the right steps toward solving "the Jewish problem" not just in Germany but also in Poland. Pilsudski's successors adopted the view that forcing the Jews to get out of Poland was mandatory to "heal" Poland. Fear began to spread among Jews when Poland actually began seeking territories to which the "excess Jews" could be transferred.

This was the atmosphere that supported my decision to sail to Palestine and try to live there for a while.

I liked the idea of defining a goal that would require me to commit to staying in Palestine for a predetermined period, which is why I liked the idea of taking part in the medical conference in April. I thought that would give me enough time to get accustomed to life in the East, not for a moment suspecting what difficulties I'd encounter throughout this journey.

Choosing the ship was no easy feat. The passenger route between Constanta and Haifa had recently become very popular. Many travelers chose this route, most of them immigrants referring to themselves as "olim" – a word connoting pilgrimage, as if they were pilgrims heading for the Jewish state. I may sound cynical, but I believe that the days of immigrating to Palestine for ideological and Zionist reasons were probably over. Most of the immigrants were simply escaping the horrendous difficulties in Poland or its neighboring countries. At the time, it was not easy to immigrate to Palestine. Receiving an immigration certificate was well-nigh impossible. The British tried to minimize immigration to Palestine, particularly from Poland. I don't know for sure whether this observation of mine was based on fact, but it was my gut feeling.

As embarrassing as it may sound, I confess that I chose the ship Polonia only thanks to its poster. It may sound romantic, but the Polonia poster caught my attention when I was on the train to Lwow to return some books to the School of Medicine library. These posters stared at me from nearly every billboard in town. They were aimed at the one-hundred thousand Jews in town – about a third of its population. It was not advertising immigration as such.

Polonia – "The way to travel"

The colorful poster promised a "coastal sail for touring and exciting experiences in the East". Sailing on this ship, especially in the first and second class, was considered sailing in style, and that was perfect for me. On the spot, spontaneously, I decided to stop by the company's office in Lwow.

"And what does the lady want?" Asked the travel agency clerk, somewhat condescendingly, because what on earth would a woman be doing on her own at a travel agency? Only when I corrected him that the "lady" was in fact a Doctor, did his expression change from condescension to wonder, as if he'd been rebuked. When I elaborated further, saying I would like to sail to Palestine in a first or second class cabin, the next hurdle presented itself: "You probably wish for a fancy cabin for you and your doctor-husband." "I am the Doctor, and I am traveling alone," I replied. "And you are right; I want a comfortable cabin overlooking the sea".

"Madam-Doctor will not have any difficulty in obtaining a visa, whether for tourism purposes or should she wish to reside in the Levant," the clerk continued after collecting himself, and hurried to add, "Those who can provide one thousand British Pounds receive their visa almost immediately." Even though the sum he mentioned was huge, I had no trouble raising it at once. And so I purchased my sailing ticket to Palestine.

The medical conference planned for April 1936 had four objectives: First, like in any professional organization, to discuss the situation of Jewish physicians in various countries. The motivation for such a discussion was the growing anti-Semitism in Germany and all other Eastern European countries. Physicians in those countries were mostly Jews, and many of them often suffered from persecution, degradation and harassment. The second objective was to discuss medical problems faced by Jewish residents of states with high-density population. Or, to put it more bluntly, to discuss Polish Jews' medical conditions which were deteriorating due to poverty, plagues, and poor sanitation in densely populated cities. The third objective was to find ways of dealing with diseases and tropical epidemics in Palestine. The fourth and last objective was to discuss the possibility of establishing a school of medicine in the Hebrew University of Jerusalem.

I wasn't really interested in most of these subjects: The politics of Jewish doctors was of no concern to me; about the diseases of the poor I knew enough; tropical diseases in Palestine were irrelevant to me; and the idea of founding a medical school in Palestine sounded like a good initiative, but not one that justified entire days of public debate. Still, I thought that the first Jewish medical conference in Palestine could be interesting, a good opportunity to meet new people with whom I'd have enough in common to enable lively conversations. Such get-togethers were very rare for me in Chortkow.

That's how I ended up in a relatively small cabin on the second deck, rocking on the waves, enjoying a cool, caressing, salty breeze. The cabin was decorated in subtle, light hues, its floor adorned with painted tiles. On one side of the cabin, next to the wall, was a single bed, its frame made of metal tubing, typical of modern German furniture. Opposite the bed there was a shelf with a mirror. A small washbasin was right next to the door; however the toilet and shower, shared by all second deck passengers, were just down the hall. I couldn't bear the idea of sharing a small cabin with a total stranger. I was very particular about my privacy, and sensitive to any light noise when sleeping. I'd be especially needful of privacy in case I was seasick, god forbid, due to stormy weather. I had no previous experience with seafaring, and that in itself was a cause of concern to me. I thought it preferable to suffer quietly on my own rather than being a nuisance to a stranger or exposed to unwanted chattering; which is why I added a considerable sum of money to have the cabin all to myself. The thought of sharing a shower and public toilet with strangers bothered me, but the cost of a fancy cabin in first class, with one's own bathroom, was beyond my budget.

Junio had promised me that, once in their apartment in Haifa, I'd have a room of my own, knowing full well how important privacy and peace and quiet were to me; so I didn't worry about my living quarters while in Palestine. From his letters I gathered that Haifa had quickly developed from a small, Oriental market-town to a bustling modern city. The surge in development and building in Haifa provided Junio with plenty of projects, and I was curious to see the international-style buildings he told me about, complete with photographs, proud of his advanced creations and his part in building the country.

I knew I'd get along fine with Junio, but wondered about his wife Malca, whom I knew to be the daughter of a rich Hassidic family, a young woman who had never worked for her living. Junio finally succeeded in marrying Malca when, after a year in Palestine, he returned to Chortkow, persisting in his determination to ask for her hand in marriage. Faced with the intensity of their love, her parents relented. I couldn't help wondering about the nature of their relationship, since Malca was in many ways the total opposite of Junio, so different from us Finkelmans.

The Finkelmans were so worldly. They were part of the Enlightenment Movement and made sure to provide their children with a higher education. They travelled frequently and were lenient in their religious attitude. The Kramers came from a very different background and culture. They belonged to the strict Stratyn Hassidic community, were rigorous in adhering to religious laws, studied Torah, and usually left business matters to the women. However, they did not provide their daughters with higher education, because they believed a woman's mission was to be a man's wife, a housewife, and possibly help with running the business.

The voyage on the Black Sea was short and peaceful. Within a few hours, when it seemed like we were heading towards the mountains, the Bosporus Straits suddenly came into view, between two hills. It was a fascinating view. We continued sailing for hours, covering around thirty kilometers, I'd say. Next to us in the water were smaller ships and fishing boats. Some had white sails, others emitted greyish-white smoke that came curling out of their chimneys, creating little clouds in the sky. Both banks of the strait were densely populated, with a mosque in every village or hamlet, their turrets pointing skyward. As we progressed, the houses seemed closer together and more cramped, the number of mosques increased, and the boats around us became more numerous and close together, to the extent that I was anxious of possible collisions. In the distance one could see Kushta, as we used to refer to Constantinople. First to become visible were the mosque turrets, then the harbor. Suddenly the straits widened. A voice over the loudspeaker announced that we'd reached the Sea of Marmara and would be docking soon. Several boats approached us from the pier, bringing supplies and additional passengers. Loading the cargo took a long time, and I realized we weren't going to disembark. I grew tired of watching, and left the deck to go to sleep and restore my energy for the second day of the trip. My fatigue and the gentle rocking overpowered my curiosity and ruminations; I fell asleep immediately. When I woke up with the first light of dawn, I was famished. Small wonder, considering I hadn't eaten since early afternoon of the previous day. At the washbasin, I gave myself a "French bath", dabbing my body with a washcloth, avoiding the shared shower for the time being. I put on a summer dress and walked over to the dining hall to try the ship's kitchen. The smell of freshly baked bread welcomed me. Each table had a basket of tempting loaves. There were two couples at the table I joined: a German structural engineer and his wife, who looked about thirty-five years old, and a couple of doctors from Warsaw, around fifty. We introduced ourselves to one another. I spoke Polish to the doctors, but communicating with the German couple was more awkward because my spoken German wasn't that good. I'd acquired some German while studying medicine, so it was mainly professional jargon; and the German couple didn't know a word of Polish. But during the conversation it suddenly turned out that we could all speak Hebrew; they were all Zionist activists from Berlin, who'd studied

Hebrew as part of their preparation for immigrating to Palestine. My Hebrew, too, was not bad; in Chortkow it was quite fashionable to learn Hebrew, and I often practiced it, especially with Junio. It was a strange feeling, to sit in a fancy dining hall on a Polish ship sailing to Palestine, conversing in Hebrew with passengers from Germany.

The coffee was excellent, just the way I liked it – boiling hot. The fresh bread was served with a large selection of cheeses, various types of sausages, cured meats, pickled herring, butter and marmalade. The problem was not what to eat but how to stop. A problem which was solved soon enough, when the loudspeaker announced that we were approaching the Dardanelles. Time to leave the table and go out on deck to enjoy the view.

Apparently, while we were at breakfast, the ship had cast off and left Constantinople. Sailing on the Sea of Marmara was very similar to sailing on the Black Sea. Once again I was amazed by the number of ships and fishing boats. Though it was chilly out on the deck, I resisted the urge to go indoors because I was enchanted by the peaceful sea with its gentle waves. After hours of tranquil sailing we reached another strait – the Dardanelles, connecting the Sea of Marmara with the Aegean Sea. These straits were wide and long, and ship traffic became increasingly busier. As the hours passed, I felt that I was leaving Europe and heading for the unknown. The wind grew stronger, the waves higher. The Aegean Sea faced us with its wrath of high winds which kept whipping rain water into the air. I escaped indoors, still watching the raging waves crashing against the ship's prow, creating a curtain of sparkling drops. For brief moments, in-between waves, dry land was visible as if the watery curtain had been pushed aside. We sailed past one small, uninhabited island, then another, then more islands. Some of the passengers near me threw up and rushed back to their cabins. The high waves didn't affect me; I was mesmerized by the stormy sea. For the first time in my life I saw a real sea, great waves breaking against the ship and splashing its deck. Some two hours later the rain let up, and fragments of blue sky peeked between the heavy clouds. Balancing myself, I walked over to a table next to a window with a view of the sea, sat down and ordered a glass of wine. I felt lonely. I found it hard to contain all the beauty of the forceful waves all by myself. Or perhaps it was the wine, making me dizzy and flooding me with still-painful memories of a lost love. Flooded by sadness, through a dreamlike haze, I heard someone ask, "May I sit down here, Madam Doctor?" I immediately recognized the Warsaw lilt in the speaker's Polish, but did not recognize the speaker. Next to me stood a tall, slim man of about forty, dressed in a fashionable suit and wearing round horn-rimmed glasses. "Yes, of course, you're welcome to join me," I replied instinctively, and regretted it immediately, but it was too late because he had already sat down. "Kindly let me introduce myself… I'm sorry, I should have done so before sitting down, but I was in a hurry to sit because of the rocking," he blurted with some embarrassment. "My name is Nathan Hoffman," he carried on, blushing, and, I must say, there was a certain charm in watching a grown man blush like an awkward teenager. "I've been watching the way you drank in the view for quite a while… and only after I succeeded in persuading the head waiter to give me your name, did I get up the nerve to approach you. I'm a representative of Culture League, the

Warsaw publishing house, but I'm originally from the Katowice area. I intend to try and get bookshops in Palestine to take an interest in the new cultural trend we represent. I'm sure Madam Doctor is familiar with the Young Yiddish group from Lodz, headed by Moshe Broderzon, the artists Marek Szwarc and Jankiel Adler; and The Gang – Die Chaliastre from Warsaw that includes Peretz Markish, Uri Zvi Greenberg and Henryk Berlewi; and surely you also know the avant-garde monthly Young Vilna by Avrom Sutzkever, Chaim Grade and Benzion Mikhtom." I was dumbfounded by this stream of names, some of which I identified as part of the modernity trend in Jewish culture. I was familiar with The Gang, because they published the works of the Revisionist poet Uri Zvi Greenberg. Junio admired his poetry and often read it to me. "And what kind of doctor is Madam?' the man asked rather impolitely, without giving me a chance to introduce myself. "I'm Doctor Syma Finkelman, a physician from Chortkow. I'm on my way to see my younger brother in Haifa," I replied. "Isn't Chortkow next to Buczacz?" He asked, and immediately went on to answer his own question, "I know those are neighboring towns, I found out only two weeks ago at a lecture I attended "A Simple Story" – you know, Agnon's latest novel, published by Schocken in Berlin. I bought the book and have it with me here on board; I've been meaning to start reading it during the trip."

"Yes, those towns are close, but the population of my town is about twice that of yours. They say that Agnon's father used to pray in the Chortkow Hassidim's small prayer house, the shtibl, until his dying day. I haven't read anything by Agnon yet," I continued on the same subject, wondering where this conversation was going.

"And what type of physician is Doctor Finkelman?" He demanded to know, looking me straight in the eye for the first time since he sat down.

"I'm a pediatrician, I have my own clinic, and this is my first trip outside of Europe."

"And is the Doctor – if I may ask – traveling on her own?"

"Yes, you may ask. The Doctor – my name is Syma, by the way – is traveling on her own, because she is an unmarried woman," I answered with a smile, and added, "Not married and quite independent." This time I, too, blushed, and it was very embarrassing. Mr. Nathan Hoffman's face lit up; seemed to me to indicate that he liked my answer.

"Perhaps you'd like to accompany me on a short tour of Athens after we dock in Piraeus tomorrow?"

To tell the truth, I'd been thinking about it while I was sitting there staring at the rough sea and the sky that was clearing up. I'd be glad to set foot on solid ground again, and I was very curious about the ruins of ancient Athens, especially the Parthenon at the top of the Acropolis. However, I didn't feel comfortable about the prospect of wandering on my own in a strange place, not knowing the local language. I debated whether it would be proper to accept Mr. Hoffman's offer, having only just met him a few minutes ago. So I said with a smile, "First let's arrive safely in Piraeus, and then I'll see how I feel about it." I regretted my answer as soon as I said it. After all, what had the nice gentleman suggested? Going dancing or an intimate rendezvous? But what was done was done and couldn't be taken back.

As we were into our third glass of wine my head was spinning, and silence replaced our repartee. Meanwhile the sky cleared up and the red sun began its beautiful descent into the sea. The sun painted the clouds red and gold, and it seemed as if even the sea itself was watching the view and settling down. While fascinated by the sunset, from the corner of my eye I scanned Mr. Hoffman's face. The sun painted it a copper hue and emphasized his green eyes. We were approaching a large island and sailed by its white houses, glowing in a gold haze.

"This is Limanos," said Mr. Hoffman, breaking the silence. "Once we pass it, the sun will set and darkness will fall," he added knowingly. "Would Madam Doctor Finkelman consent to dine with me? She is on her own and so am I; this way we'll be able to use only one table, since the tables are set for two... And besides, I'm enjoying Madam's company. Madam hasn't asked, which is why I didn't say anything, but maybe it's time to say that I am not married. The crew on the ship knows me because this is my third trip to Palestine; so we could sit at the Captain's table, if that would suit you better?"

Once again he managed to make me feel self-conscious; I wasn't accustomed to such directness from strange men. But I was enjoying his company, so I retorted, "Thank you, I'd be happy to accompany you to dinner, but there's no need for the Captain's table. I'd prefer a quiet evening to a multitude of people chatting." After a slight hesitation, I added, "Let's meet in thirty minutes at the entrance to the dining hall."

Half an hour later I was striding towards the First Class dining hall. I assumed that Mr. Hoffman, for whom this was a business trip, ate in this hall; especially having been invited to the Captain's table. I smiled when I saw him leaning against the dining hall doorway, chatting with the Head Waiter, from whom he had apparently gotten my details. I immediately noticed that Mr. Hoffman had changed his shirt, and replaced his necktie with one that happened to be of the exact shade of blue as my dress.

"Good evening, Madam Doctor Finkelman," Nathan greeted me with a wide grin, bowed briefly, took my hand and kissed it lightly, his lips barely touching my hand, in the Warsaw fashion. The Head Waiter led us to a table at the very end of the dining hall, next to a window. Contrary to Nathan's earlier words, this was the only table in the entire hall which was set for just two people. Obviously this was no coincidence. Mr. Hoffman was making every effort to impress me.

"Would Madam prefer fish or meat? I personally prefer fish. The fish were freshly caught this morning, in the Sea of Marmara. The meat is from Romania. Should you order fish, we'll have white wine, and should you prefer meat, we'll have the red. All the wine here, as you've probably noticed, is very good; all from France." I laughed aloud and replied, "I think I can rely on your judgment, considering how you so exquisitely matched your tie to my dress. I assume you're good with details, and besides I always prefer fish, even though I'm more familiar with freshwater than with saltwater fish." Mr. Hoffman laughed too, and assured me, "the waiter will debone the fish, so that you're not faced with that chore." He gestured to the nearest waiter, and to my surprise spoke to him in fluent Italian, which was totally unintelligible to me. My Latin was of no use to me in this case.

"Let's settle something. I'll join you on the trip from Piraeus to Athens, and in return you'll stop addressing me as Madam Doctor Finkelman. You can call me by my name, Syma, and if you find that difficult, then Miss Syma as is customary in Poland." This time I got him to laugh. "I think Miss Syma will come more naturally to me; what can I say? Apparently, I belong to the older generation." He was definitely amused. The waiter returned, a bottle of white wine in one hand – Maison Louis Latour Chablis, 1935 – and a silver plated, Art Deco jug to keep the bottle cold. The waiter uncorked the bottle and let Mr. Hoffman taste the wine. "Wonderful wine," said Mr. Hoffman approvingly, "I think Madam will enjoy it very much." This time he spoke Romanian. The waiter proceeded to pour the chilled wine into our glasses, then quietly walked away.

Along with the wine came fresh bread and butter, followed by the appetizers. The waiter served the sliced vegetables and the selection of fish with his left hand, while his right arm was held decorously behind his back. He bent slightly to enable me to select from the appetizers. I looked, and froze in my seat. From among the vegetables and pickled or smoked fish, tiny squid and small crabs looked back at me. During my studies in Lwow and on my many trips to Warsaw and Vienna I didn't bother keeping kosher. But shellfish, which the Bible scorns as disgusting creepy-crawlers – were too much for me. Mr. Hoffman must have noticed my distress and hastily came to my rescue. "Madam Doctor Finkelman is allergic to shellfish," he explained to the waiter, then proceeded to select some fresh and pickled vegetables and a few pieces of smoked fish, which weren't right next to the creepy-crawlers, and placed them on my plate, looking straight into my eyes and saying with a smile, "Welcome to the Mediterranean Basin. Over here we eat anything the sea can give us and, personally, I find it all delicious. I think this is a good occasion to enjoy our first glass of wine." Long after, I would recall this moment as the moment I fell in love with Nathan. Within a split second he turned from Mr. Hoffman to simply Nathan, the man I loved.

From that moment on, the evening became wondrous. I have no idea what I ate… I think it was a tender, filleted white fish served with roasted potatoes, but I'm not sure. The wine, on the other hand, I shall always remember. It was cool, smooth, flavorful, and head-spinning. I recall that we talked a lot, laughed our heads off, though I can't remember over what. I called him Nathan, he called me Syma, gone were the Mister and the Madam. I remember him helping me reach my room, and then politely apologizing that his head was spinning from the wine, and leaving. Disappointment cut as deep as the desire. Months later he came clean and said, "Yes, it was difficult for me to leave you that evening, particularly after we did away with the Doctor and only Syma was left. But we were both intoxicated, and I wanted us both to clearly remember and cherish the moment …" Have I mentioned already that Nathan was a real gentleman?

A splitting headache and stinging embarrassment flooded me the next morning. Before I had a chance to start feeling sorry for myself, I heard a knock on the door followed by Nathan's confident voice: "We'll be reaching Piraeus in an hour and a half. Let's meet in half an hour for morning coffee, where we sat yesterday." Without waiting for my response, he walked away. I could hear his heels clicking on the wood floor. I washed myself quickly; chose a comfortable, not too-formal dress, and flat-heeled shoes which I'd brought for my touring of Palestine. I parted my hair in the middle as usual then combed it back and up into a French twist, so as to accentuate my long neck. I powdered my cheeks and nose, in an attempt to tone down the blush that flooded my face each time I thought of last night.

Nathan was sitting in the colonnade with his long legs stretched out comfortably, exuding self-confidence, a steaming pot of hot coffee and two cups on the table in front of him. He had been concentrating on the view through the window – the shore strewn with dozens of white houses. As soon as he saw my reflection in the window he turned, stood up and took my hand. "Good morning, Miss Syma, I hope you slept well and that your headache isn't as bad as mine," he said with a fine smile. "I slept well, my head indeed aches, I guess we drank a little too much last night. I trust the coffee I smell will do us good," I replied, looking him straight in the eye. He brought my hand to his lips and kissed it gently. "First coffee, then plans for the rest of the day," he said, and led me to the armchair overlooking the view. Coffee, fresh white bread, butter and delicious strawberry jam did wonders for me. The fact that the sea was calm also contributed to my feeling of wellbeing. I was excited at the prospect of travelling from Piraeus to Athens with such a good-looking, charming man, about whom I knew so little. The ship was sailing between blue skies and clear water, towards the houses on the horizon. The loudspeaker announced that in about an hour we'd reach Piraeus Port, and instructed all passengers who planned to disembark to take their passports and a form confirming them to be "Polonia" passengers, to make sure they'd be allowed back on the ship. These papers were provided to the passengers at the ship's office.

"No, I don't have a suitable hat for strolling around town. I do have several hats packed somewhere in my suitcase, but they're for cold weather. I didn't think I'd need sun protection. I know it sounds silly, but that's what I have, or rather, what I don't have," – was my reply to Nathan's question whether I intended to don a hat once we disembarked. "You could use one of my two Fedoras. One is grey, the other dark burgundy. I think they'd fit you because your hair would fill any gap," he said with a mischievous smile.

I laughed but politely declined. "I'll buy one in town if necessary. This might be a good opportunity to buy a straw hat, which I believe will prove useful in Palestine."

And so we found ourselves walking up the Acropolis, he with his fashionable Fedora and I with my wide-brimmed straw hat which caught my eye as soon as we exited the harbor. It was my first purchase since leaving Chortkow. Nathan wore khaki cotton trousers and a short-sleeved button-down, no tie, and his round horn-rimmed spectacles that sat just beneath the rim of his hat. We looked like your everyday tourists, which indeed we were. Along the way, coachmen offered to take us to the Parthenon in one of their decked-out carriages, but we turned them down. We preferred to make the trip up the hill on foot. We started our tour at the spot where the taxi driver dropped us off. Nathan had asked the driver to take us to the open-air Theater of Dionysus just south of the Parthenon. I was taken by its perfection, couldn't believe it was built in the fourth century B.C. North of the Theater stood the tall Parthenon, an amazingly beautiful construction of columns. We climbed our way in that direction, enjoying the cool breeze on our faces. "It's far better to climb this hill in May than in the middle of summer, under the blazing sun," said Nathan, and continued to tell me about his first time, two years earlier, that he'd climbed the Olympus. I couldn't help wondering whether he'd been on his own, or perhaps with a woman or a friend, but I didn't dare ask.

"On a clear day, with good visibility, you can see Haifa from the Acropolis," he suddenly said, as we were breathlessly climbing up the hill. "I gather it's a bit like being able to see Warsaw from Piraeus," I joked. It's rather funny, how such a silly phrase stayed in my mind many years after Nathan was no longer in my life. When going through dark and difficult moments in my life I'd recall this phrase, and somehow it made me smile, cheer up or find solace. It became my mantra: On a clear day, with good visibility, you can see Haifa from the Acropolis."

I suddenly remembered the last time I saw a photo to do with the Acropolis. It was during one of my visits to see Junio in Vienna, about seven or eight years ago. There was a magazine lying open on a table in the room of one of Junio's friends. On the open page was a beautiful photo of a barefoot dancer by the Parthenon columns. I learned that the dancer was Isadora Duncan, a trailblazer in modern dance. She was killed in a traffic accident in France that very year. When I told Nathan about this photo, I was surprised by his answer: "That series of pictures was taken by Edward Steichen, a Vogue fashion photographer. I saw one of the photos from that series in Berlin two years ago. A publishing house specializing in avant-garde art was thinking of publishing a book about Isadora Duncan, as a tribute, five years after her death. I don't know whether such a book was ever published, but if you're interested I could find out."

"It would be nice to get a copy of one of these pictures; I remember them as being extraordinary and, from now on, they'll have an additional significance," I said. We continued walking uphill, fascinated by the Parthenon as it was gradually revealed to us in all its glory. A huge structure with eight magnificent columns, topped by a symmetrical gable which, though partially ruined, enabled one's imagination to complete the missing parts. The structure stood on a hill, elevated above its surroundings, supported by a steep wall. We had to go around the wall from the left in order to reach the entrance to this gigantic edifice.

This was the first time in my life that I'd ever seen such an ancient and impressive structure. Until that day, the oldest buildings I had seen were the castles, fortresses and palaces of Galicia, some of which dated back to the early sixteenth century, but they all paled in comparison to the beauty of the Acropolis. I was undergoing a strange experience: I was sitting on a huge rock, probably a relic of an ancient structure, next to a good-looking man whom I'd met only two days earlier and already felt as if he'd always been by my side. We sat there and watched the scores of tourists climbing the hill, with scenic Athens as backdrop. For a moment I felt out of place, in a foreign setting, as if I were on the outside, watching a scene in a movie. There, near the Parthenon, I first felt desire for Nathan. "I wish we could, right here and now, on this rock…" I fantasized.

"Let's go down and find something to eat before getting back to the ship", Nathan said, interrupting my thoughts. Indeed, my stomach was rumbling with hunger; it was only the presence of Nathan by my side that had distracted me. Nathan led the way downhill. We descended first westward, then walked north of the Acropolis and to the east. The steep drop at the north prevented us from climbing straight down into the Old City, which Nathan referred to as the Plaka. The Old City was a web of alleys and narrow streets.

The Parthenon, 1935

Nathan led the way through those small alleys with the confidence of a person knowing his way around and, about a quarter of an hour later, we were right in front of a restaurant surrounded by multicolored geraniums. "This is the Sholarhio restaurant, belonging to the Kouklis family," Nathan said. "The restaurant opened only this year. I was here about a year ago, when it was still under construction. I got to know the Kouklis couple on a night out with friends, enjoying music and drink."

We sat at a corner table next facing the view of the narrow street, or possibly alley, next to a lush red geranium bush, its flowers glowing in the sunlight. To my great surprise a steady flow of assorted starters arrived at the table, before we had a chance to decide what to order. Small dishes with food the likes of which I'd never seen. The colorful fare and the abundance of vegetables were different from anything I knew. This was the first time I had Greek food. The flavors, too, were so different from what I was used to. Some were on the salty side, some sour, and others stingingly spicy. In Chortkow we weren't accustomed to eating much fresh vegetables, aside from cabbage; most of the vegetables were eaten cooked or pickled. The hot, spicy flavor of some of the dishes was unfamiliar, but after the initial surprise I was relishing the culinary experience.

How could I not? Together with the assortment of dishes, arrived the Chief Wine Steward, an older man, tall and lean, wearing a red vest embroidered in black over his dark clothes, and holding a bottle of a clear alcoholic beverage. "This is Ouzo," explained Nathan while the wine steward poured some into my glass. As he added ice cubes to the glass, a kind of magic occurred, as if thin smoky clouds emanated from the ice and gradually painted the clear drink white. My expression must have given away my surprise, since Nathan reacted humorously, "Don't be fooled, the drink has not turned into milk, it's still very strong." We clinked glasses and toasted to a successful journey. I didn't care for the drink; I immediately identified the anise flavor, but out of politeness continued to take very tiny sips. The food, however, was delicious, and I enjoyed savoring the new, unfamiliar dishes which continued to arrive at the table. The Ouzo did its job, after all. The tiny sips I took apparently accumulated to make me quite dizzy.

"I've had quite enough," I said to Nathan apologetically. "No need to continue this banquet," he said. "Sixteen empty dishes and one empty Ouzo bottle testify that we must have done a good job!"

I got up, somewhat wobbly, and leaned on Nathan's solid arm. Outside the restaurant a cab awaited us, having managed to squeeze its way into the alley. I sat next to Nathan and rested my spinning head on his shoulder. I may have even snuggled next to him. In any case, I remember that the trip was pleasant. I felt it was too short, because, in my opinion, it should have lasted at least an hour.

I don't remember how we reached our cabin on the ship. I'm not even sure which cabin it was. I don't know how I got undressed, and whether Nathan helped me. All I remember is a tangle of arms and legs, with me clinging to him and he pushing his body against mine. It was a passionate storm, the memory of which still makes me smile. I knew that the ship was still anchored and that this storm existed only between the two of us. I had never known such passion in my life, and when he entered me I was ready for him.

I don't dream much. Or more accurately, I hardly remember my dreams. Perhaps it was the alcohol or maybe it was the night's events and emotions which my brain processed and transferred to a different location, culture and time. I didn't dare open my eyes for fear that the dream would vanish; I just wanted to withdraw back into sleep, into the sort of eternity I was floating in, half-asleep.

I remember very clearly the moment in my dream when my cup of tea was empty, and the sensation of my tongue as it touched the bitter remaining tea-leaves transported me to a different reality.

People were beginning to move about along the opposite bank of the canal. In a few minutes, the village would be bustling. She loved the morning sounds, the children running cheerfully down the road, full of renewed energy provided by their night's sleep; the voices of the farmers urging their water buffalos on the way out to the fields; the voices of merchants unloading their fresh vegetables and other wares. Nanshe had woken up.

It was market day, her favorite day of the week. The air was full of the aroma of spices, colorful fabrics glittered in the sun, and the smell of incense wafted over from the row of temples. She loved watching the crowds who came to the temple to seek information – or to at least get a momentary glimpse into the future; she liked to contemplate those who put their faith and their fate in the hands of fortune-tellers, star-sign readers, palm readers or face readers. She loved watching those who came to inquire about loved ones, to seek blessings, wish for means of making a living, or seek comfort in promises of better days to come. She loved watching those who came carrying fortune-sticks, then stood or kneeled in front of the temple door, devotedly shaking their wooden tube of fortune-sticks until one stick sprang out, having freed itself from the rest. Then they'd pick it up from the ground, cautiously and anxiously, studying the lucky number on it. Some knew by heart the meaning of all hundred sticks; others hurried with the stick to the fortune-teller's stall, expecting him to interpret and provide comfort or encouragement.

Her pupils began assembling. She saw them plodding heavily towards the center of the village, as if the commotion of the street had nothing to do with them, was not part of their world. She could identify them by their bearing. She was amazed by the change in them; within a few weeks they had mutated from light-footed mischievous boys, skipping and running down the road, to introverts following a slow inner rhythm, as if all their energies were directed inwards. Their slowness stood out in contrast to the lively hubbub of the street, and their white garb, so different from the customarily colorful market, disconnected them from the village life.

He joined her and they left the house, she dressed in crimson and he in white, and together they crossed the wooden bridge over the canal and walked over to the group of pupils. Like a procession of white ants they were, with the pupils in their footsteps, heading out to the rice paddies at the end of the village. There they stopped, under a huge bo tree. She sat down under the tree. The pupils addressed her by her name, Nina. Yumin was at her side, the pupils in a semi-circle in front. The scene may have looked odd to random onlookers because people sitting passively in a field, doing nothing, was an unusual sight in this agricultural area, especially people dressed in all white. But to the residents of Nanshe this was not unusual. Teachers and their pupils were an inseparable, important part of their life. They were part of the community and were an honor to the village. Everyone in the village was familiar with the carved achievement-tablets – tall granite stones, placed at the temple entrance by the region's clerk, at the ruler's command, as testimony to the pupils' scholarly achievements, for the next generations. This was a custom practiced by the rulers of the Ming dynasty, to commemorate and glorify the village's spiritual achievements, as part of their aspiration for perfection.

The pupils were sitting with their eyes closed, clearing their minds, breathing with deliberation so as to prepare themselves for the lesson. Then, each pupil in turn, when ready, stood up carefully, took a few slow steps, stood before the teachers, took a small bow and returned to his place. Throughout the entire morning ceremony not a single word was uttered; the only sounds were those coming from the marketplace, and the tweeting of birds in the field.

"A person building his home ought to take an example from the rock on the ground," she said, opening her morning talk. "A rock stands with no pretense, knowing

its place. A painter ought to observe the humbleness of the leaf, and the singer should listen with humility to the song of the bird, its precision of sound and volume; it does not presume, does not hesitate, and therefore has no difficulty singing.

"The idea is not to reduce and restrict, because that creates discomfort. The idea is humbleness. Man should aim for humbleness. And, what is humbleness? Humbleness is when one places oneself as equal to the experience. Neither superior to it nor inferior to it, connected to oneself and equal to one's own existence. Where there is love, there is humbleness, containment, then absorption. There is no need to define boundaries and feel deprived or satiated. The feelings both of deprivation and of over-satisfaction result from lack of love; love for one's self. Because loving the other stems from loving the self. The ability to contain love without the need for measuring it stems from confidence in self-love. The ability to love several people and to be loved by many people stems from letting go, flowing, not hanging on. Because the calm person is like the rock in the garden, secure in its place, feeling part of the environment, beloved by the universe, and feeling neither too much nor too little."

The sun began setting. They sat both surprised and hypnotized by her words. She seemed like a high priestess in an ancient ceremony. For a moment it wasn't clear whether it was her dress painting the sky red or whether it was the rays of the setting sun. The sound of her voice entered their hearts, through their equanimity straight to the emotions which they'd gotten used to hiding so well. It was unexpected. For many days she'd been following them with her eyes and her silence, and today she opened up with speaking and singing. Her singing sounded like a choir of angels, full of sorrow and happiness, animation and serenity that enveloped them with softness, embraced them, and they were taken in by her love, and she in theirs. The sound of her voice was like no other singing they had ever heard. For them it was a hymn, a song of longing for a different place, a place they did not know, as if she had presented them with a sublime riddle that was insoluble to humans. Then suddenly she stopped. And the sun, which earlier had stopped its setting at the sound of her voice, hurried to catch up and disappear. Silence prevailed. The crickets were first to break the silence, followed by the frogs, the night birds and the wild animals. The pupils remained seated for a long time, reluctant to get up, hanging on to the memory of her singing. Together they began walking silently; they did not speak any more that evening. Then they dispersed, one by one, each going his own way, enveloped quietly by the darkness.

I woke up serenely into the quiet after the storm. Remnants of the enchanted dream were still in my thoughts when I noticed that the cabin was different. It was more spacious than mine, and the room was awash with blue from the clear, cloudless sky seen through the large window. Nathan was sitting in an armchair opposite me, wrapped in a dressing-gown embroidered with the ship's crest in gold, immersed in a book. This is what traveling first class is like, I thought to myself, taking in the large, airy room, while my dream was gradually beginning to fade.

It was embarrassing to wake up in a room other than my own, next to a strange man. Good looking and impressive, but nonetheless a stranger. I was as naked as the day I was born, covered only by a thin sheet. Nathan was still reading, unaware that I'd woken up. From the corner of my eye I saw my clothes, neatly folded, on a table next to the bed. I felt a certain relief – at least I'd be spared the awkwardness of having to look for my clothes.

"At some point you'll have to stop pretending you're still asleep," Nathan said in his calm, confident tone. "I'm embarrassed," I replied, my face turned away from him, escaping his gaze. But then I felt his hand softly caressing my head. His touch took me by surprise; I hadn't heard him move. I must have been too focused on my embarrassment. His touch was pleasing. Days later I told him that during those few moments I was at a loss, and only when he suggested that he'd leave the room and we'd meet for breakfast a short time later, did I regain my senses. He left, and I had a wonderful shower in his ensuite bathroom, trying to figure out the meaning of my strange dream. "So, this is what it's like in first class... being able to enjoy a morning shower," I said and grinned to myself.

For a moment I thought the ship had cast off, but it must have been just a slight giddiness induced by the hot water. So I turned off the water and helped myself to a large, soft towel. I put on the same clothes I'd worn the day before, which were in good shape, not even smelling of perspiration, despite our long trek of the previous day. That deodorant cream Ethel sent me from America did wonders. It was the only item she used to send to me occasionally, together with her answers to my letters. I made sure to always include a twenty-dollar bill because I knew she could not afford to pay for my whims, and would find this sum helpful. Anyway, I rushed to my cabin to spruce myself up. After a brief hesitation, I decided to change into something else, as if to open a new page. Or maybe I wanted to appear to be a woman who is in control of her life, a strong woman who doesn't brood over yesterday. This attitude had prevented me from developing a regular relationship with a man many times in my life.

Nathan was waiting for me at the entrance to the dining hall. I smiled uncertainly at him. "I'm glad you're joining me for breakfast, Doctor Finkelman," he whispered to me while bowing slightly, taking my hand tenderly, bringing it to his lips and kissing it fleetingly. "I gather we're starting anew," I answered good-naturedly, "let me introduce myself. I'm Syma, a well-educated but flighty woman who is easily seduced by good-looking, striking men." This time it was Nathan who was at a loss, unsure whether to accept the compliment or deal with the cynicism. But he quickly found his voice and said, "The pleasure is all mine; I'm pleased to enjoy your company in both spheres: the one of intellect and the one of playfulness."

We looked at each other, then burst out laughing. The tension evaporated, as I melted into his piercing eyes.

We were seated next to the physician couple from Warsaw, whom I was introduced to on the first day of the trip. They asked if I'd gone on the organized tour of Athens. When I told them I had a very enjoyable tour with a private guide, Mr. Hoffman, they stirred uneasily, lowering their gaze, since they knew I was traveling on my own. During breakfast, the Polonia sounded its horn and set sail.

We were two totally different people, Nathan and I. I am a woman of average height, my body nice and round without being voluptuous. My facial features are somewhat manly; I wear my hair parted in the middle, usually pulled back and tied up, revealing a long neck. I have a mind of my own, am assertive, stubborn and independent, though also capricious and given to mood-swings. I must admit I am not always pleasant company.

Nathan, on the other hand, was tall and slim, nearly ascetic-looking. He was good-looking with a chiseled jaw. His hair black, wavy, and slightly greying at the temples; his posture and bearing aristocratic-looking. His green eyes were like two gleaming emeralds set in his tanned face. He was always well-dressed, and his dark horn-rimmed glasses accentuated his bright eyes. Nathan was also highly knowledgeable, and apparently knew his way around women. And so he won my heart.

I'll never fully understand the nature of our connection. We were so different, yet so mutually complementary. Possibly it was desire, the desire that had been hidden so deep inside me, and which he was so good at bringing out. As days went by, we became attached, but at the same time we both needed our privacy and separateness. Possibly because I was not by nature a docile, subservient woman, who gives in to her partner's will and loses herself for his sake.

During the Mediterranean journey we were preoccupied mainly with the question of how I should present Nathan to my family. Obviously, I didn't want to be perceived as a reckless woman who jumped into bed with the first good-looking man she met on the ship. Even though this "jump" seems to have turned out very well.

So we came up with what we considered a plausible story: Nathan and I first met in Lwow, at the travel agency where I bought the ticket for sailing to Palestine. An acquaintance of three months, for two adults, seemed a reasonable time in which to develop a relationship serious enough to live up to conservative standards. The more complex issue was finding an answer to the question, which was bound to rise, concerning the future of our relationship; particularly in considering that Nathan had planned to stay in Palestine only a month, whereas I hadn't limited the length of my stay. We agreed to give the answer that was closest to the truth: Nathan intends to leave but return according to his work needs, we will take it one step at a time, and… time will tell.

The voyage aboard the ship was like a honeymoon of a couple who wasn't officially married: we kept two separate cabins, but in practice shared the bed in First Class. I'd go to my cabin in Second Class only when I needed, say, a change of clothes or a cardigan, or some essential item. I preferred to keep my suitcases in my own cabin so as not to clutter up Nathan's neat, comfortable cabin, and I suppose also to ensure I'd be able to escape to my private quarters if necessary – something that did not happen throughout the entire voyage.

Every day Nathan would read to me, in Hebrew, a chapter or two from Agnon's novel A Simple Story – about the tragic life of Hirshl Hurvitz and his unrequited love to Blume; how, through matchmaking, he married Mina who stole his sleep, or rather his ability to sleep at night; and how he went mad, and later recovered. I was fascinated by the story. At some point it sounded to me as if Agnon was talking about Chortkow, not about Buczacz (called Szybusz in the story) where the plot takes place. I could easily imagine the characters, whose description sounded just like people I knew in my own village, some of them even from my own family. I could nearly hear my mother saying this sentence which Nathan read out to me: "A bachelor can be free to follow his heart, but what would the world come to if he didn't put his romances aside when the time came to get married? A fine place it would be if everyone followed their hearts! I wouldn't envy it." My mother used to lecture me in similar words, whenever I refused to hear of a shidduch, an arranged marriage, and used to warn me that I'd remain an innocent old maid all my life. When I shared this warning with Nathan, he said, "Well, we both know your mother was wrong, you are definitely not innocent…"

Within two more days of sailing I learned many more things that hadn't been part of my world heretofore. I learned to drink Campari and soda, got used to its bitter flavor and enjoyed it. I learned to eat and to enjoy raw fish sprinkled with only salt, lemon juice and olive. I learned to expose my body to the sun in the presence of Nathan, without feeling shy or self-conscious – though only in his cabin, by our window, not in public. And I learned to surrender myself to Nathan's endless caresses.

***

Palestine

We were awake for most of the night, and with the first light of day we could see it: the coast of Palestine.

It was undoubtedly the most beautiful sight I've ever seen. Through the morning mists we saw Mount Carmel, towering in all its glory above the sea, as the Polonia quietly approached it. The sea was calm, free of waves, as if made of polished crystal. Once every few moments, as if at a set rhythm, a gentle ripple painted a white strip on the blue water, then melted away, as if not to interfere with the blueness of the water. The right side of the mountain sloped steeply down to the sea, leaving a narrow strip of beach. The mountain's left side continued uninterrupted towards the horizon.

We sailed into the large bay, the ship's bow heading towards the mountain, which got bigger by the minute. I could easily see houses on the slopes of Mount Carmel. On the ridge there were very few structures, two or three of them very close to the right-hand slopes.

"This is the Stella Maris monastery, meaning "the star of the sea", Nathan explained. "And the structure on the right houses the Lighthouse of Haifa. The monastery used to be the palace of Abdullah Pasha, the ruler of Acre in the 19th century. The present lighthouse was built thanks to a donation of the Spanish Consul." Most of the houses I could see were in the center of the mountain, on its lower half, as if setting a goal for Polonia to reach.

My heart was racing with excitement. Either because of the breathtaking view, or perhaps because of the unknown I was facing, compounded by a certain anxiety: Junio was expecting me to be on my own, definitely not with a man at my side.

It was quite clear to Nathan and me that, sooner or later, our ways would part. I intended to stay in Palestine for at least a year, maybe even consider building a future there for myself; whereas Nathan came for a predetermined short period, to promote his business. He was completely open when expressing his skepticism at the prospect of selling a significant number of books in Palestine. According to him, the flourishing of the market for books in Palestine was on the decline, and selling just a few hundred copies of a single book was considered a success. He concluded that there was no correlation between the increase in population due to the waves of immigration to Palestine and the state of the book market. "Maybe that's an inevitable result of the many different languages of those immigrants. After all, people prefer reading books in their mother-tongue," he used to say. On the other hand, a constant, continuing growth in population was a source of hope. "In five or ten years' time," Nathan speculated, "these immigrants will speak Hebrew, think in Hebrew, dream in Hebrew, their children will study in Hebrew, and the book market will finally flourish. Who knows, maybe it will eventually be possible to make a living in Palestine as a bookstore owner, selling magazines, periodicals and newspapers along with stationery and writing utensils, as the Steimatzky brothers are doing. They've opened stores in Tel Aviv, Jerusalem, Haifa, and even in Beirut. But I have no interest in this type of work; it lacks soul." What didn't lack soul, according to Nathan, was the process of bringing a new book to life – a process he had told me about the previous evening.

But I was preoccupied by other concerns: How should I introduce Nathan to Junio? As a man I met on board the ship and into whose bed I hastily jumped? Or as a friend or boyfriend from my Lwow university days, whom I happened to bump into on the ship, or at the travel agency – our original plan? And it would be obvious that I'd want to make use of this opportunity to spend some time with him before he goes back to Europe.

Nathan sort of made the decision for me, by saying half-jokingly, "But we do know each other a long time. Maybe not strictly in years, but definitely in terms of how we feel." And so I imagined us disembarking as old friends, who happened to meet again after years apart. But in reality I was ill at ease, and more than that – anxious about my privacy. Nathan was supposed to stay in Haifa for a few days of business meetings. He had a reservation at the Zion Hotel, a new, modern hotel, which he said was close to Haifa's new residential area and within walking distance of the Finkelmans' house. Finkelman House – Beit Finkelman as it was known in Hebrew – was at number six, Nordau Street. The house was constructed by

Junio for Heidi and Herman Finkelman, a rich family from Vienna who closed down their business due to the mounting anti-Semitism and decided to "make Aliya" to Eretz Israel and settle in Haifa.

"If I want to visit you at your brother's place it will require considerable effort, because it's all uphill. But should you decide to come see me at my hotel, you'll find it very easy because it's all downhill. As for getting back – we'll sort it out together," Nathan joked.

While the Polonia was approaching the port, we decided that it would be best to disembark separately and, later on, find a way to connect with each other. To be more specific, we agreed that I'd phone the Zion Hotel once I settled in at Junio's place.

I was standing on the top deck when the Polonia made its way into the harbor accompanied by a tugboat. I shuddered as the ship blew its horn. The loud sound pierced my thoughts, and I turned to look at the shore. The pier, which looked like a continuation of the streets behind it, was crowded, busy and noisy. On one side stood dozens of horse-drawn and donkey-drawn carriages, and on its other side trucks of various sizes. Along the pier an assortment of men were rushing back and forth in a frenzy, some of them wearing strange oriental garb, the likes of which I'd never seen before, others were in British military or police uniforms, or in suits. They seemed to me like kids playing some imaginary game. In sharp contrast, there was a different group – men and women, who stood motionless, probably waiting for the ship and its passengers.

I strained my neck, I squinted, but couldn't see Junio or Malca in the crowd. A heavy apprehension seized me. It wasn't fear of not finding Junio; I was confident that he was there, waiting for me. It was fear of the unknown, concern over the encounter with a new, strange country. I was uncertain about my professional future in this country, and concerned about possible violence between Arabs and Jews.

I was obviously at a crossroads. Would disembarking lead me to a new life? Would it disconnect me from my old world, as it did for Junio, enabling him to create a new life, far away from his family? My entire life, so far, I'd walked a predetermined route. I knew from a young age that I would become a physician. Wanting to become a doctor is what drove me to excel in my high school studies, and graduating cum laude enabled me to be the first Chortkow woman to be accepted to medical school in Lwow. The desire to practice medicine brought me back to Chortkow in order to open my own clinic, against all odds: the first private clinic owned and run by a woman, a clinic that began prospering after just a few years of hard work. And, hard work it was indeed. I felt I was suffocating: long working hours; living at home with my mother; the lack of privacy; and life in a small town where everyone knows everything about everyone else – all those closed in on me. So the voyage to Palestine seemed like a getaway, even if only a temporary one.

The view of the approaching pier, the smoke exuding from the trucks, the booming noise of the ship's engines, the loud voices of excited passengers, and – more than everything else – the hustle and bustle on the pier, all enveloped me and made me wonder whether Palestine was indeed the right alternative, the right place for me to begin a new life. There was always another alternative. For example, the United States of America, to which my sister Ethel had moved for good, some eight years earlier. But life there was far from a bed of roses, particularly after her architect husband left her for another woman. She lived in New York City's Lower East Side, worked as a dressmaker under conditions not too far from slavery, and earned a meager living. True, there was no comparing her circumstances to mine. She was a deserted wife, a poor dressmaker, whereas I was a well-to-do physician. But her depressing letters, expressing her loneliness and sense of "no way out", deterred me from seeking my future in America.

There was also a more exotic option… to try and seek my luck in Colombia, South America. My brother Chaskel, who'd moved there, kept in touch, wrote every once in a while, describing the amazing scenery, the abundance of business opportunities for people of education and means, and the dire need for doctors. He went into detail in his letters to me, about his business, his achievements so far and his dreams for the future, including in the latter the possibility of establishing clinics and hospitals in the hope of drawing me there. I loved my brother Ezekiel, but his obstinate, hard-headed temperament was too much like my own, which used to lead to prolonged, draining fights. The mere prospect of such fights caused me to nip in the bud any possibility of moving to South America.

Of the five Finkelman offspring, Junio was considered the most even-tempered, easy-going person. Though he, too, could be stubborn, compared to his siblings his stubbornness was bearable. We forgave him his idiosyncrasies, maybe because he was the youngest. Moreover, I knew him to be reliable, so when he invited me to come stay with them in their new home in Haifa, I knew he'd do everything he could to make me feel comfortable. There was a small community, perhaps a few dozen, of Chortkow people in Haifa, some of them youngsters who were related to our family. I thought that their presence, the knowledge that they were nearby, would help me – the newcomer to this foreign country – to maintain a social and cultural connection with familiar aspects of my life.

During all the commotion and loud honking, the ship finally docked. Only then did I finally identify Junio and Malca standing in the crowd, their eyes scanning the passengers on board the ship, trying to find me among them. I would never forget that moment. I felt as if I was an onlooker, a spectator watching a movie. Junio and Malca looked happy together, arms around each other, as if the hubbub surrounding them had nothing to do with them. Only their heads moved left and right, unsuccessfully trying to find me. A short while later, as I was pushing and being pushed on my way down the unsteady steps, I heard Junio's voice, calling out loud in Polish: "Syma, stoimy tutaj!" – Syma, we're here! Seconds later I felt myself lifted up in his strong arms. A long hug later, we took a step back to take a good, curious look at each other. Only then did I notice that he'd lost a lot of weight. The new look suited him. Next, Malca hugged me; "Welcome to Haifa and to Palestine!" she greeted me in Hebrew. "We hope the voyage wasn't too hard on you."

I was standing on the sticky, grease-stained pier, trying to ignore the stench of the horses, and suddenly felt the ground moving under my feet, as if I were still onboard the ship in mid-sea. Junio took my arm and supported me as he led me towards a nearby warehouse, where he promptly sat me down on a chair to recover. I don't know whether it was the excitement, the stench, the very bright sunlight I wasn't used to, or the abrupt move from the rocking ship to terra firma that caused my dizzy spell; but a glass of cold water quickly helped me recover.

We stood in line for the British immigration official, the Representative of the Crown, as Junio referred to him jocularly. The line moved very slowly, and it seemed to take forever until I was finally at the official's desk, answering his questions.

"I've come for the conference of Jewish doctors that is to take place in April in Tel Aviv, and of course to visit my family who lives here in Haifa. I have no intentions of staying here, I have an active medical practice in Poland and I intend to go back there after my visit." I spoke the truth, even though I was open to making changes in my life. The visit was more a checking out of the territory, than an action, ahead of making a decision. To my surprise, the official nodded in understanding and approved an unrestricted stay, though this did require a medical check-up. It was obvious to me that the British were following the quarantine laws, taking preventive measures against infectious diseases, particularly tuberculosis. Later on I gathered that I'd been lucky: many of the ship's passengers were arbitrarily separated from their families and put in quarantine. Some of those who were healthy to begin with contracted infectious diseases while in quarantine.

I was restless. Then the penny dropped: since the moment I'd set foot on the ground, I hadn't seen Nathan. I gave one last look at him before disembarking: he was standing, leaning on the ship's railing, looking at the shore, as if watching a play enacted below. For a moment he turned and looked at me, smiled, then looked down. Since that moment, I hadn't seen him. I tried to find him in the long line of passengers lining up for border control, but in vain. I looked back, but my field of vision was blocked by all the people around me. For a split-second I thought I saw him walking into the arrivals hall but, just then, the Immigration Official ordered me to continue on my way to the baggage hall.

Such chaos I have never seen in my life. Piles of suitcases, footlockers, huge wicker baskets, thousands of crates and other types of luggage, surrounded and interwoven by a huge, loud, frenetic crowd. It was the strangest crowd I'd ever seen: British clerks dressed in suits; seamen in navy uniforms, dark-skinned Arab-looking porters wearing white, black or red keffiyehs, and in-between distraught passengers trying in vain to locate their luggage. And the stench! That was the worst of all. The smell of rotting food, horse dung, and sour sweat. I ran out of the large hall, trying to get some fresh air into my lungs and curb the awful nausea that overcame me.

"Welcome to Palestine – land of new odors, where the sunlight hurts your eyes", said Malca, with a sympathetic little smile. "Living here isn't easy, but I believe you'll get used to it." She took my arm and showed me to a lone bench outside the building. "Let Junio locate your luggage; he's experienced and just ignores the noise and the smells."

Malca and I sat for a long while on the bench in the shade, protected from the intense sun. I gave Malca the latest news from Chortkow, telling her about the many who want to leave Poland because of the economic difficulties and the increase in anti-Semitism, but who can't afford to buy a visa to Palestine nor to pay for the expensive ocean voyage to the United States of America. "Shortly before I left," I told Malca, "I met your parents by the bazaar in Chortkow. They were walking around with your brother Moshe, and Pepe, your adopted sister, who's grown to be quite a pretty girl. They wished me a good trip and asked if they could give me a small bundle of letters for you, from your family and friends. It's in my suitcase, of course."

Malca was delighted. She then told me how much she missed her parents and her girlfriends, and about the loneliness she's been suffering in Eretz Israel. "Honestly, I feel like I'm under siege. The days are all alike. Juno leaves for work early, gets around town, inspecting the construction work of new projects in Hadar HaCarmel, the city's commercial center; or else he's in the office with his business partner. He gets home after dark. I would love to find employment, but Junio won't hear of my going out to work, as if it's beneath us." She went on to tell me about the small Chortkow community and the other Finkelmans who live nearby; about her women-friends whom she meets to play cards with in the afternoon, once she's done with house chores and cooking. She went on and on, describing her life, evidently relieved to have someone to confide in; while I was too tired to continue listening. I was sitting there, melting in the heat despite the shade, for a moment at a loss to understand what on earth I was doing here, on the pier in Haifa.

Suddenly, I heard his voice, its familiar lilt breaking through my reverie. "Hello, Madam Doctor Finkelman," he said in Polish, I wanted to say goodbye before leaving the port. I've already found my luggage and even found transportation to Hadar HaCarmel. I wished to tell you how much I enjoyed our conversations aboard the ship, and that I'd be happy to see you again." I felt my face flush, and not from the sun. I hastened to introduce Nathan to Malca, trying at the same time to catch my breath. "Mr. Hoffman is a salesman for a Warsaw-based publisher. We met in Lwow, and later became friends on the ship." It all seemed perfectly clear and simple to Malca, who reacted quickly, "Great! And who will you be staying with?"

"Not with whom, but where," Nathan answered pleasantly. "I'll be staying at the Zion Hotel." Malca happily retorted, "Oh! The hotel is not far from us! Just about a half-hour walk up the mountain. We'd love to have you join us for dinner tomorrow night; it's Shabbat eve, you shouldn't be eating alone in the hotel." "Thank you very much, Mrs. Finkelman," Nathan replied graciously, "I'd be delighted to come, and delighted to meet your husband, about whom I heard quite a bit during the voyage." Malca gave him their address, 15 Hillel Street, and added, "We'd be happy if you came in the afternoon, if possible." As if she'd read my thoughts.

And so, out of nowhere, things fell into place and my first meeting with Nathan in Haifa was arranged. At that moment, I couldn't care less about the heat, the stench seemed to dissipate, and Haifa no longer seemed like such a horrible place.

Actually, Haifa turned out to be a newly-built city. Most of the houses I saw were built of cut stone, next to cement and white stucco buildings, of a plain, undecorated design. I easily identified the building style – Junio had described this modern style very well in his letters. From every point in town you could see the mountain, and the houses that seemed to be climbing up towards its peak. Any car on the winding street had a hard time climbing uphill… that was evident from the black smoke it left behind. But more than anything I was impressed by the old olive trees I saw everywhere, along sidewalks and in people's yards. It was the second time within a week that I ever saw olive trees. But compared to the ones I saw in Greece the ones in Haifa were larger, their trunks all twisted and gnarled, wrinkled like the face of an old man. The strong sunlight made their leaves shine in bright green and silvery hues. I loved the look of those trees, and was delighted to find them in Junio and Malca's yard.

The men in Chortkow would never walk around town dressed in shorts; nor would the women ever wear pants, not even elegant slacks. It was considered inappropriate: shorts were only for children, and long pants were only for men. Imagine my amazement when I first saw – even before we left the harbor area – men and British soldiers wearing shorts; and later – women in pants.

Hadar HaCarmel and Haifa Bay, 1935

The landscape totally took my breath away. The higher the taxi clambered up the mountain, the wider the view was of Haifa Bay. Out on the horizon, the blue sea touched the azure sky; the red roofs of the houses were as picturesque as an artist's brushstrokes. Most of the new buildings had flat, white roofs, whereas the old houses had red-tile roofs, so it was easy to tell the new parts of the city from the old. The unbuilt slopes were covered in rocks, bushes, olive trees and cypress trees, completing the beautiful scene.

Halfway down the mountain stood Junio and Malca's home. It was quite clear that all the houses on that street were only recently built. They all had flat roofs, large balconies, and square glass windows and wooden shutters arranged symmetrically, evenly spaced, on the front. All railings and fences were made of simple bent pipe, as if there were some unknown entity that had forbade any decorative elements. I wasn't sure I liked that style. The plain, non-decorative houses seemed bare, and exposed the architect's lack of creative talent for all to see. Apparently, only the most talented among architects could create an aesthetically pleasing minimalist style. But I kept my observations to myself. Junio, on the other hand, could not stop raving about the wonders of the city of Haifa. He talked about its fast development and the many new projects being built. In particular, he spoke about Hadar HaCarmel neighborhood, which was to be a "garden city", based on the plan made by architect and town-planner Richard Kauffmann in 1922. Similar to the new concept of Achuzat Bayit near Jaffa, the garden city was supposed to be a residential and academically oriented zone, clean of pollution and commercial areas. "This is a great opportunity for all of us to demonstrate what we know, to take part in building thousands of houses that will house the thousands of immigrants that are sure to arrive. We're building a new city in Haifa, which is why most of us prefer to distance ourselves from existing architectural styles – the Arab one, the Oriental one, and even the British style – and build houses in the new aesthetic style, similar to what is done in Tel Aviv," he explained enthusiastically. There wasn't any way I could curb his enthusiasm by expressing my opinion that some of said houses looked bare, as if there wasn't enough of a budget to allow for proper building.

Their apartment was small: two bedrooms, a small kitchen, and a living room with an adjacent dinette. The bathroom and toilet were two separate rooms. Though it seemed as if much thought had been given to making the most of the space, still, in Chortkow terms this apartment was tiny and looked more like students' quarters in Lwow than a family home. The apartment had a large balcony overlooking the bay, and when Junio saw my astonishment at the size of the balcony relative to the rest of the apartment, he explained: "The balcony is not an indulgence. It's the most airy and pleasant place on hot summer nights. This is where people eat and host their guests, especially when the heat indoors becomes unbearable. You'll see what it's like, in a month or two from now." I laughed inwardly; Junio often knew what I was thinking even before I knew it myself.

"I gather we have a guest coming over for dinner tomorrow," he went on. "Malca told me you have a new beau, a good looking guy from Warsaw who knows a thing or two about books." I blushed, but answered without blinking, "Well, that's what happens when adults traveling on their own meet in the moonlight. It's easy to make friends."

We had tea and sandwiches as a light lunch, then Malca helped me unpack my suitcases and put my clothes neatly in the wardrobe. With the curiosity of a teenager, she checked the labels on my clothes and asked if she could try on a few of them. We had a good laugh – my clothes were way too big for her, and looked as if they were draped on a hanger. Malca had a slim, girlish figure, which suited me fine, since I didn't like it when others borrowed my clothes, as my sister Zelda used to do occasionally.

Once this stage of my settling in was over, I gave Malca the bundle of letters from her family and friends, and I thought this meant that in the next few hours I could relax in my room, finally on a solid bed that didn't move to and fro with the waves.

But Junio had other plans. He wanted to hear about our home in Chortkow, about family and friends, as well as about the political climate in Poland. I knew this would mean stepping into a minefield, considering the sharp differences in our political views – I was active in the socialist HaShomer HaTzai'r movement and Junio being a right-wing Revisionist. So I began yawning and rubbing my eyes, until he gave up on continuing the conversation and let me go to sleep.

I lay in bed covered only by a sheet. The bedsprings hummed a quiet tune and the moon peeked from between the cracks of the shutters. I couldn't fall asleep. The empty space beside me in bed wouldn't stop taunting me. "Too much space here…" I mumbled to myself. I felt lonely. The bed in the next room was singing a love-song, or perhaps it was the springs of all the beds in the building, or in the entire street. More than anything, I missed Nathan.

For many years I'd been accustomed to loneliness, calling it "privacy". I couldn't bear the thought of sharing my bed with another person all through the night, hearing his breathing and smelling his body. I liked to sleep naked in a large bed under a cool, smooth sheet, in a cool, dark room. But here, in Haifa, at the end of the world in a foreign place, in a street where the beds were squeaking their songs of love, I missed the feel of Nathan's body next to mine.

I lay there restless for a long time. I don't know when I finally fell asleep – probably at early dawn. When I woke up, the sun was high in the sky.

The smell of cooking greeted me as I opened the bedroom door. The world smiled at me, but I escaped, wrapped in a sheet, to the shower. The hot water erased my thoughts.

Thus, without any plans, began my new day in Haifa. There was no one home. Several steaming-hot pots stood on the cooking range. On the dining table I found a note in a round, childlike handwriting: "Junio is out. Coffee and tea are in the left-hand cabinet next to the stove, the bread is in the breadbox, the milk in the fridge. I'm going downtown to get onions and lemons, which we're out of, and challahs for the Sabbath."

It was my first breakfast on the balcony overlooking the gorgeous view of Haifa Bay. A plate with a sandwich cut into triangles, a cup of boiling hot coffee and a cool sea breeze were the perfect menu for my first morning in a faraway land. I curled up comfortably in a wicker armchair, hand-made by a local Arab craftsman, watching the street below as if I was watching a play from the balcony of a theater. The noise coming from the construction site down the road, where a group of men were working on the scaffolding of two houses, caught my attention. A cacophony of Arabic, Yiddish and Polish filled the air, and the torsos of the suntanned, sweaty men glistened in the bright light.

When Malca came back, the slamming of the front door woke me up from my snooze. She was carrying two big shopping baskets. She caught her breath and smiled at me: "Walking there is fine, and takes some twenty to thirty minutes, all downhill. But the way back is uphill, and is quite demanding, especially around noontime when the sun is blazing hot," said Malca, in reply to my idea of going down and paying Junio a surprise visit in his new office. "Besides," she added, "it's Friday today so everyone finishes work early, and I don't even know whether Junio is in the office or on location, supervising construction sites."

So instead, we both went out for a short walk along Hillel Street. We walked eastward along the street, across the mountainside. I needed to stretch my legs, and Malca was happy to join me for a while even though she'd only just gotten back from shopping. I was surprised by the extent of the new building going on. It looked as if the new houses were trying to rise and overtake the top of the mountain. It reminded me of the big construction push in Chortkow in the twenties, an effort that was quashed by the political and economic crisis.

In between the trees and houses, some of them still under construction, I could see a breathtaking view of the bright blue bay. I could see a few ships sailing towards the horizon, leaving behind a black trail of smoke. For a moment I thought the Polonia had sailed, too, but then I noticed it tied to the pier. It's not too late to run back home, I thought for a minute. Am I scared of the unknown? I had no answer. Time would tell.

After a short walk we reached a spot where the road intersected with a very steep road leading to the left, straight from the mountain to the sea; and just opposite it, to the right, stone steps led steeply up Balfour Street. We chose to continue uphill, while Malca jokingly counted the steps in a mixture of Hebrew, Polish and Yiddish: "Achat, dwa, drei, arba, pięć, zecks, sheva…" and so she went on until we reached one hundred and eight steps, at the corner of Bar Giora Street. The higher we climbed, the sparser the buildings became, and the vegetation changed as well;

the olive trees nearly disappeared, replaced by low shrubs covering the rocky slopes. Breathing heavily, we stopped, in awe of the view in front of us. "Just look how far we can see!" Malca exclaimed. "Over there, at the edge of the bay, is the ancient Muslim city of Acre; and the white strip behind it, along the horizon, is the chalk cliff of Rosh HaNikra, marking the Lebanese border. You can get there by train. If we can persuade Junio, maybe we can travel from there to Beirut, they say it's an enchanting city, full of French restaurants with high quality food!" said Malca excitedly, carried away by her plans.

As for me, I was thinking about the sea; I'd never actually bathed in a sea. Neither in salt water nor in a sea with actual waves. We sat down at the top of the stairs, trying to squeeze under the shade of a fig tree, to escape the sun. "And where are the bathing beaches?" I asked, and Malca elaborated: "There is the big beach, called Khayat Beach, but it's on the other side of the Carmel mountain range. And there are the Bat Galim beaches, which you can see to the left of the port. The best one is definitely the Khayat family's beach, where you can both bathe in the sea and eat in restaurants along the coast. But it doesn't matter much to me because I can't swim. Junio tried to teach me, but I'm scared. No one in my family can swim, I think it's genetic in our family... whereas you Finkelmans are swimmers, we are totally useless when it comes to water."

We were beginning to feel thirsty and decided it was time to go back home. I found it hard to believe that only two years ago there was no seaport here, nor did most of the houses I saw below, on the mountain side, exist.

Going downhill was easy, and within about fifteen minutes we were already on the balcony, sipping cool lemonade that Malca made out of the fresh lemons she'd bought, and cold water from the refrigerator. Suddenly it sank in that there was no ice box in the fridge. It was an electric refrigerator! Malca noticed my surprise and said that her parents had bought it for them, and added: "In the old part of the city you can easily have ice delivered to you, but there's no way to persuade the iceman with his horse and wagon to come here… It's too hard to make the horse climb up the mountain, not worth it in order to sell some ice… But we have a reliable supply of electricity, so the food doesn't go bad."

Soon enough, Junio came home. I saw him as he entered the building, heard him skip up the stairs and dramatically open the door. "Hi, my bourgeois brother," I greeted him happily, "An electrical refrigerator, no less! And I thought life in the Holy Land was hard!…"

"Syma, don't forget we're living in the twentieth century! We cook on an electric range, we keep our food cold with electricity, we even heat water for our shower with electricity. Who said this country isn't modern?" he said teasingly. "But a telephone is a different matter. Not a chance. Maybe in five or six years' time this part of town will have phones. Even in the office I don't have a telephone, and am reduced to using our neighbor's, Dr. Blumenthal's phone, which makes it a bit awkward for clients who must call the clinic of a psychiatrist… but it's the only telephone in the building, and we're not going to get one any time soon."

"Obviously, Haifa isn't Chortkow," I pointed out, "there,

with a bit of cash, the wait for a telephone line would be greatly shortened."

"We have to start getting ready, remember, we have a guest for dinner!" Junio announced on his way to the shower, after downing a whole bottle of cold water.

"Relax, everything's prepared, I just have to set the table. We'll have plenty of time to get ready after we've all showered," said Malca, then added while winking at me, "Just remember that two more people have to shower after you, so please don't use up all the hot water."

Of course we had to shower in whatever hot water there was left, just as we did in Chortkow, so it was in Haifa; the Finkelmans' world remained the same…

Nathan arrived at six o'clock sharp – the knock on the door sounded just as the clock struck six. I felt my cheeks flushing and my chest heaving. Junio opened the door and sized up Nathan with one glance. Sized up, and smiled, as if approving my choice.

"Welcome, any friend of Syma's is a welcome guest," he said graciously, shaking Nathan's extended hand while accepting the proffered flowers with his other hand.

"Actually, we're the only ones who haven't been introduced yet. I'm Junio, Syma's younger brother. Let's go sit on the balcony until we're called to the table."

Junio brought a bottle of Fine Champagne, his favorite Stock Brandy, accompanied by a small dish of thinly sliced herring with lots of onion and a plate of crackers. The three of us made ourselves comfortable on the balcony while

Malca excused herself and went into the kitchen to put the last touches on dinner. The brandy eased the initial awkwardness, and within minutes Nathan and Junio found plenty of mutual interests, while I listened and observed, the alcohol gradually taking effect and mellowing my thoughts. They talked about the thriving construction business, but shortage of professional workmen; discussed the fact that construction was not, traditionally, a Jewish occupation, but the huge need for skilled workers provided an opening for vocational training, leading to a reliable source of income for many. From there, the conversation naturally continued to the various workers' unions and the conflicts between the Revisionists and the unionized socialist workers. To my relief, they sailed through this loaded topic smoothly. The Fine Champagne may have had something to do with it. The conversation started out in Yiddish and Hebrew, but as they drank, they slipped into Polish. "I guess drinking in Polish comes more natural to them," I thought to myself. I must have been deep in thought because Nathan had to address me twice, saying, "Come, Syma, we're being called to the table."

Junio made the Kiddush over the wine and said the blessing over the challah, as was the family's custom in Chortkow. Malca had told me that, since our father's death two years earlier, Junio made a point of keeping these customs, as if assuming the responsibility for maintaining the tradition.

Nathan, relaxed by the brandy, asked: "And why do we cover the challah?" To my own surprise and everyone's amazement, he immediately answered his own question, in an exaggerated Yiddish accent, as if joking: "Generally speaking, as we all know, the Seven Species with which the Land of

Israel was blessed are: wheat, barley, grape, fig, pomegranate, olives and dates. Should a man eat two or more of these foods, he must eat them in the same order as they are mentioned in Deuteronomy. Since the two types of grain are mentioned before the grapes, one must eat the bread before the wine. Therefore, we cover the bread, which is made of wheat, so as not to "embarrass" it by the fact that we are drinking the Kiddush wine, made of grapes, before eating the challah, made of wheat." He then quickly added in his normal voice, "This is a remnant from the education I received at the Jewish school. Over the years I've moved away from tradition, but apparently some things stay with you."

Malca served a bowl of chopped liver which was a delicacy. Chopped liver, fresh challah, pickled cucumber and wine were a combination I could not turn down. Whenever I ate this sort of Polish chopped liver, I always thought of my dear departed grandmother and the way she prepared it: She had a heavy frying pan which was used chiefly for this purpose; she gently stirred the chopped onions on a low flame, never taking her eyes off them, to make sure they reached the exact desired golden color, without burning, God forbid. Then she would add the livers and stir them with the onions slowly, to keep them juicy. Then she'd add a tablespoon of sweet red wine and a bit of salt and pepper to improve the flavor. When the mixture cooled down, she would chop it up, stir it again, and immediately serve. Malca's chopped liver tasted like home.

I helped Malca take the plates off the table and bring the main course: roast beef, boiled potatoes, and sweet carrot tzimmes, as befitting a Polish meal. The food was perfect. Malca had prepared it all early in the morning, before I even woke up. We ate quietly, enjoying the delicious food. Nathan obviously felt at home, and was the first to ask for a second helping. He joked with Junio and complimented Malca. "Better not rely on public transportation if you want to be on time for such a good meal," he said.

"Transportation is not the best aspect of living in this part of Haifa," Junio agreed. "It is indeed difficult to find a taxi or a carriage to Hillel Street, even in daytime, not to mention in the evening, and definitely not at night. I walk to the office in the morning and come back on foot in the evening, neither of which is much fun in summer nor in winter. The bus service is improving, and they say it will soon reach the corner of our street. But for this to happen, City Hall must first complete paving the streets, especially the ones going up the mountain."

Malca and I served the tea and the Mandelbrot almond cookies she baked. I watched Nathan and Junio chatting as if they were old friends rather than two men who only met a couple of hours ago. Malca seemed quite taken by Nathan and whispered to me in the kitchen in Polish: "On naprawdę przystojny", meaning "he's a really good-looking man." And I blushed immediately, giving myself away as usual.

"See you all tomorrow at Herman and Heidi's. I'm going with Nathan to his hotel and there's no point in my coming back here before the visit." This statement, made spontaneously, was suddenly out there, stunning all, though I was completely determined to take this daring step.

Though I was by no means a young girl, and nine years older than my kid brother, Junio, I could tell by the stunned expression on his and Malca's faces that they apparently hadn't understood the nature of my relationship with Nathan, and were at a loss to respond. Actually, I must have surprised Nathan, too. He was obviously taken aback, stirring uncomfortably, not knowing what to do. It had never occurred to me, not for a minute, that this was not in keeping with his plans.

Junio tried to break the ice with his typical sense of humor: "Nathan, welcome to our family." Nathan laughed and answered, "Looks like I've been accepted quite easily." Only I, who had initiated this unexpected move, remained discomfited.

We left, with Malca and Junio walking us as far as the corner of the street. Hillel Street was pitch black, except for the full moon that showed us the way. We said our goodbyes and exchanged kisses on each other's cheeks, then continued down Balfour Street. Nathan carried my bag, with my toiletries and a change of clothes, his other hand around my waist. So we walked down towards the city lights. I was sure that my heart was thumping loud enough for all to hear, only there was no one but us on the street. The darkness became thicker. I would definitely not have dared to walk there alone. As we passed the campus of the Technicum, Nathan stopped, put down my bag, took my face in both his hands and kissed me a long, slow kiss. "You must be crazy, Madam Doctor Finkelman," he whispered in my ear, "You most definitely gave Junio and Malca much to think about... You surprised me as well, but I am so happy with your choice." I kissed him back, closely wrapped in his arms and by the darkness of the night.

We continued downhill, crossed one well-lit street and then another, and within minutes reached the hotel. It was nearly ten p.m. The hotel's façade was well lit. It was a modern structure, like most of Haifa's newer buildings. Atop the high-ceilinged ground floor and mezzanine were three residential floors surrounded by large balconies. Nathan's room was on the top floor, under the rooftop bar. The clerk at the reception desk smiled at Nathan and greeted us with "Good evening". I think we looked like a respectable couple ending their day's tour in a foreign country. But, in fact, I was emotionally tense in anticipation of my adventure, and didn't bother to wonder what I looked like to the receptionist.

Nathan was the perfect lover. I could easily give in to his caresses, which is just what I did. His touch elicited from my body sounds that I didn't know it could make. I was trembling, and not from the cool air. I snuggled up as close as I could to his body, as if escaping from my own thoughts. I was confused. What was going on? Was it the distance from Chortkow? These new surroundings? Or had I simply morphed within a week into a reckless, shameless, wanton woman, driven by lust, living her life like there's no tomorrow?... Whatever it was, I surprised myself by the ease with which I waved off these thoughts, and drank in the scent of his body. I took him into me and we became one.

Was this merely the beginning of an adventure, a stormy relationship bursting into my life like a wild wind, wiping away memories of unrequited love and betrayal? Or was it the first act of yet another impossible love story, a relationship limited by time, with no horizon and no future? But why bother myself with such doubts? Why must I analyze and justify it to myself? Why not just let go, giving my body that which it longed for? And I was so thirsty for love, for lovemaking, without questions, without responsibility, without qualms.

We continued our mutual caressing, time stood still, we couldn't stop; towards dawn he entered me again.

At first light we fell asleep.

Saturday. A new day in Haifa. Silence outside. The peace and quiet so different from back home. A quietness accompanied by the tweeting of birds, undisturbed by anything else. No Sabbath noise of worshippers walking to and from synagogue, no noisy children playing in the street. By my watch, it was eleven a.m., and still the street seemed to be asleep.

The family plans for today were to meet for lunch at Heidi and Herman's on Nordau Street. "Number six, Nordau Street is about a ten-minute walk from the hotel, so please come for lunch, because we're invited, too." That was the last thing Junio managed to say to me after his initial shock and before parting.

I clearly had to accept the invitation, but I couldn't imagine getting up the courage to go there on my own, and face the inquisitive looks and inevitable questions about my acquaintance and relationship with Nathan. I thought Nathan's presence would curb the onslaught of questions. Or at least that was my hope. Nathan was not eager for a second family visit within less than twenty-four hours. "However… I don't really have anything more exciting to do this Saturday, and at least there's bound to be good food there," he quipped. But it was his next idea that really struck me: "How about if, in return for visiting your Viennese family you'll join me on a brief trip to Lebanon? I'm supposed to meet with the Manager of the Steimatzky branch in Beirut." I thought he must be kidding. But when he saw my skeptical expression, he added hurriedly: "Next week I'm supposed to meet in Beirut with Steimatzky's shop managers there. They wish to produce travel guides to Syria and Lebanon, and are searching for a European publisher to produce their books. We believe there is a market in Europe for such books, since the Middle East has become a desirable destination for holiday travelers from Europe. If you have no set commitments for next week, it would be nice if you'd join me. They say Beirut is a fascinating city, a kind of Haifa–for-Advanced-Tourists," he grinned at me.

I was stroking his hair, wondering to myself how come this man entered my life. I, who am so accustomed to a routine life in Chortkow, where everything is well-planned and well-known in advance… Suddenly, before I've even had a chance to settle down in Haifa, I'm already considering "popping over" to Beirut as the lady-friend of a charming man.

We stayed in bed petting and snuggling for a long time, until hunger began to gnaw at us. It was too late for breakfast at the hotel anyway, so we decided to give up on breakfast and wait for lunch at Heidi and Herman's.

The house at number 6 Nordau Street was very impressive. It towered above most of the other houses on the street, and its windows shone brightly in the sun. We got there after a slow stroll, with me gazing in fascination at all the new, modern houses along the way and the majestic Carmel. I was so absorbed by the view, that only Nathan's strong arms prevented me from tripping and falling a few times.

Herman and Heidi's apartment was on the second floor. The stairwell and the steps were all light-hued Italian marble. The wide stairwell, Junio later explained, was designed for the future elevator. There were windows all the way down the façade of the stairway, which flooded the space with bright daylight, and looked ornamental from the outside.

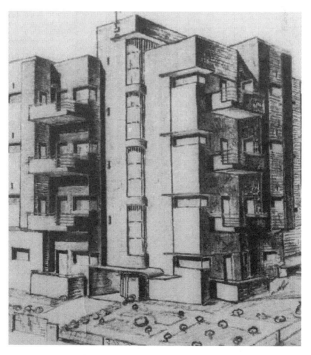

Drawing of the Finkelman House – 6, Nordau, Haifa

Handrail made from bent pipe, Haifa 1935

Junio greeted us at the door, and immediately introduced Nathan to Herman and Heidi, speaking German to them. Heidi apologized for not knowing any Polish, and not having had a chance to learn Hebrew yet, but also mentioned that she was surprised at the large number of German speakers in Haifa, which helped her manage. "Maybe my Yehuda will teach me; he's been studying Hebrew at school. They say one's children are the best teachers," she said, as she introduced her fourteen-year-old son to us. As we switched to small talk, Nathan did not seem the least perturbed; he fit in naturally, easily switching from Polish to fluent German. Malca waved at us from the kitchen, throwing a casual Hi in our direction. I gathered that it was Malca who was in charge of lunch. As it turned out, Heidi knew nothing of cooking. She was used to a different lifestyle, a life where she was surrounded by cooks and maids.

Junio showed us around. The apartment was quite impressive, very clearly designed with attention to detail, and using the best materials, all imported from Europe. The floor tiles, the porcelain tiles in the bathroom, the sinks and faucets, the windows and shutters – everything was of a high European standard.

But in contrast to the modern design of the building and the apartment, the taste guiding the choice of furniture, especially in the parlor, seemed a bit ridiculous to me; it was conservative, bourgeois, as if belonging to a different life – a life that was interrupted in Vienna, and transferred to Palestine. The expensive, neo classical furniture in brown and black, and the huge crystal chandeliers would have been more appropriate to a Vienna palace than to a three-and-a-half room apartment in a developing city, in a country still searching for its identity.

We sat down in the parlor and the conversation immediately turned to the situation in Europe and the surge of anti-Semitism. Everyone blamed the economic crisis for causing the anti-Semitic devil to rear its ugly head. Herman, who had closed down his business in Vienna, liquidated all his considerable assets and moved with his family to Palestine, said in a confident tone: "The present wave of anti-Semitism is different than previous ones. Austria and Germany are creating a new anti-Semitism, bred by fascism. It is unlike the traditional, religious, central-Europe anti-Semitism. Fascism will be the disastrous undoing of European Jewry; but unfortunately most of my friends in Vienna won't admit it. I tried to convince the Wechslers – Heidi's family – to come with us, but their answer was the standard one: things will change soon enough, and one doesn't change one's country as if it were a pair of socks."

Junio supported Herman's attitude and said he couldn't understand how Austria's intellectuals, including some of the Jews among them, could support Austrofascism. "The well-to-do find it difficult to pick up and leave. It's not easy to do what Herman and Heidi did. They sold a large textile business with excellent clientele, including the top fashion house Schwestern Floge, the Floge Sisters, for example. They left economic prosperity, gave up a comfortable life and Vienna's cultural life, to come here, to the Levant." Junio looked around, expecting reactions, and when none came, continued: "It doesn't matter if the motivation is Zionism or fear of anti-Semitism. In either case, it takes great courage to take such a step. For us youngsters it's easier. True, we left behind families in Europe, but we must admit that we didn't have much to lose. We're all still in the early stages of our careers."

I listened attentively to Junio's words. Was he trying to get a message across to me, hinting that my future should be here? Or is this a message mainly aimed at Malca, in view of her difficulties in adapting to Haifa, having given up the comfortable life she enjoyed in Chortkow as the daughter of a rich family. Nathan's voice soon broke into my thoughts: "Palestine is not the safest place in the world, either," he commented. "I don't think the local Arab population wants us here. If we're looking for a safe place, then maybe the United States or even Australia are worthwhile alternatives. Fact is, the majority of the people who have immigrated here, the Olim, as they refer to themselves, arrive here because of the economic crisis in Europe rather than being motivated by Zionism. I myself am not at all certain that I'd have the desire and the energy to start a new life at my age, especially while giving up the European culture we are so accustomed to." I was quick to identify Junio's expression when he was about to enter a political argument, so I was quick to butt in cheerfully: "I don't know about you people, but I'm starving. Also, as a doctor, I can tell you unequivocally that one must never carry on political arguments on an empty stomach."

The food was great. Home cooking: chicken soup with noodles, followed by cholent with kishkeh, hard-boiled egg, and a delicious cabbage salad. I admired Malca's cooking skills. When we'd said goodnight the previous evening, I noticed additional pots on the cooking range, but I had no idea they were for today's meal. For a while, everyone was busy enjoying their food. But the peace and quiet did not last long. As soon as we finished eating, Nathan got the discussion going again by commenting: "I guess it all boils down to money, and the ability to obtain immigration certificates either to Palestine or to America. Obviously, it's cheaper to travel to Palestine, but the difficulty of getting the British Mandate to issue a certificate prevents a mass immigration from Poland to Palestine. As for the United States – they make it easier for you only if you have an education, a sought-after profession, or if you're rich."

Junio was quick to respond, but to my relief not in an argumentative way. "I believe it's easier to move to a place where you have family or friends. In Haifa, for instance, there are about thirty families from Chortkow, and many more will come if they can only get certificates. There's a shared feeling here that we're building a new city and a different society than the one we had back home. There's no doubt that our willingness to help friends and family settle here is a factor in their decision to come, but since getting a certificate is not easy it obviously limits the numbers of those who actually arrive."

I finally decided to add my opinion: "Immigration involves a very egotistical element of exchanging one's old life with a new one while giving up one's close family and friends. In fact, the younger generation, when emigrating, are leaving their adult or elderly parents as a burden to those relatives who chose not to emigrate. It isn't only a matter of the elderlies' ability or inability to make a living, but of day-to-day caring for elderly parents and those who aren't well. Malca's parents are relatively young, healthy, and of financial means. But our mother is all alone after Father passed away. She is older and not in good health. That's why it was very difficult for me to make the decision to come here. Had Zelda not taken it upon herself to help Mother and hadn't urged me to go, I don't know whether I'd have been able to leave Chortkow for a long time."

This must have been too personal a statement, because my words were followed by complete silence. I hadn't meant to criticize anyone in the room, but Junio's expression was proof that he'd been hurt and felt scolded. So it was a relief to all when Yehuda chose this moment to demonstrate his command of Hebrew. At fourteen, Yehuda had been studying at the Hebrew Reali School nearby. All studies at the Reali were conducted in Hebrew only. After school hours, Yehuda spoke German with his parents. Herman remembered some Hebrew from his school days at Jagielnica, a small town near

Chortkow. Heidi didn't understand any Hebrew, nor did she show any interest in learning it. Junio was only too happy to change the subject, and began talking to Yehuda about his studies and his after-school social activities. I wasn't very interested in this topic and preferred to help Malca in clearing off the table and doing the dishes in the kitchen. I was bothered by the fact that none of the men had even offered to help; and Heidi, the lady of the house, behaved as if this had nothing to do with her, and sat in the living room as if she were a guest in her own home.

***

Second Dream

Sometimes life, or our insights about life, can change because of some trivial thing like a pair of underwear or the need to change clothes because you're not comfortable wearing the same clothes you wore the previous day. That's what happened to me. After lunch at Heidi and Herman's, I went back to my room at Junio's place because I didn't have enough clean clothes to enable me to stay another night with Nathan at his hotel. Nathan walked me to my room, and we said goodbye after making a date to meet at the hotel the following afternoon, after his business meetings.

And then it happened. That night I had a dream. It was long and detailed. I didn't know any of the characters, nor the story, nor the setting. I had a strange, somewhat scary feeling that the dream had to do with a distant past of mine, or perhaps the future. But the weirdest thing about it was that it seemed to be a continuation of the dream I had on the night I first slept with Nathan. I experienced a sort of déjà vu.

She was different from all other women in the village, if only by her tall figure and narrow waist. They used to refer to her as the noblewoman, maybe because there wasn't any other woman quite like her. Her long, flowing, black hair set her apart, like a signpost stating "I am here". She was a mystery to them. Her habit of not chatting with people and not gossiping set her aside. Nonetheless, they all knew that in time of need, when in anguish or distress, or when undergoing emotional turmoil, they could always count on her to lend them an ear and an open heart. She was the best of listeners. Many preferred consulting her rather than going to the village doctor. She never told them anything about herself nor boasted of the medical education she acquired in the capital. She was the only educated woman in Nanshe, a woman who chose a modest, simple life, far from her parents' home. A woman who left behind a life of luxury to follow her love. She was the one who taught him the secret of silence, the secrets of deep contemplation, and he reciprocated with love, and more than anything else – a wondrous friendship. He longed to hear her singing again, and waited for days on end.

He experienced extreme loneliness, yet a sort of pride mixed with melancholy filled his heart. He could not fathom these emotions. She had touched the most delicate chords of his being. When she sang, she seemed to him the most unachievable goddess. And even though he knew she had chosen him over all others, it gave him no consolation.

That evening, after she spread a thin mattress on the floor of their small room, she dreamt a dream both weird and enchanted: They were drifting downstream on the troubled water of the river. He was sitting on a boat shaped like a large tree-trunk. On the boat there *was a basket of apples. He was sitting relaxed, hands on his knees, wearing a golden robe, a blue, traditional headcloth covering his head, his white beard grown long, his eyes on the horizon. Next to him, on an old tree-trunk boat, were the servants: a guard with a sword on his back for defense purposes; a master flutist, a poet who writes lyrics, and one sailor to navigate the convoy, watching the horizon. Behind them, a waiter was skipping from wave to wave, holding something strange, perhaps a songbird, perhaps a cooked dish.*

And behind them all, she floats, on a huge lotus leaf. She is a young, pretty woman, in a turquoise robe, her cheeks rosy, her eyes focused on him – he who is sailing ahead of her. Next to her, a maid holds a staff with a bowl of fresh fruit.

When she woke up in the morning, she remembered every detail of the dream. Both the dream and its meaning: The Eight Immortals are celebrating her consort's birthday, blessing him with good luck, abundance, and a long life. Feeling whimsical, she imagined that perhaps, some day, in a different time, she would be lucky and see her dream come true.

That day, during class, she explained to her students that every person has a need to immortalize his existence through creation. She told them that – contrary to common belief – buildings, paintings and statues, or even ancient paintings on rocks, were not created in order to enrich or add beauty to our lives. They were more likely created in order to place signposts in front of us so that, should we return here, we would be able to recollect and recall that we've already been here in a different life. Perhaps that was the intention of the ceramics artist from Guangdong, China, when he drew his own image in the center of a painting without even knowing why. Maybe so that, one day, we would recall that he was here. Eventually, the painting was hung in the main temple, to ensure that the village would be blessed with abundance.

She was amazingly good at understanding the many possible sources of pain, and the ways to be freed from it. She fully and accurately understood the structure of the powers of one's soul. She could clearly distinguish between the thoughts of the mind and the wisdom of emotions; between memory and thought, between knowledge and sagacity, between intention and will. She wrapped up all these insights into a philosophy, which she taught her students. Once a week she sat them down under the ficus tree, while Yumin went down to the field with the tea bushes and lychee trees. She would sit and look into their flustered gaze. They were young and unaccustomed to a woman's eyes, which seemed too penetrating, entering their innermost soul. Only then, after she had scanned each and every one of them, did she begin her talk. That day, she spoke about the soul's weariness, and reproached them for looking for easy ways to reach equanimity. Meditation is not the solution to distress, she said. Your soul is full, your cup runneth over. Nor are good thoughts and light-hearted banter enough to clear your mind of thought. Only on the basis of cleansing will you be able to build a new existence – clean and pain-free.

For example, she went on to explain, imagine a thirsty wayfarer whose bottle is full of rancid water. He thinks to himself, why don't I pour out some of the dirty water and add clear spring water. The same goes for you. You have to cleanse yourselves, empty all your old thoughts. Not your knowledge, only your thoughts. Just as the wayfarer must empty his bottle, pouring out all the rancid water before refilling it with fresh spring water, so must you rid yourselves of your thoughts, and with them the pain, too, shall disappear.

She spoke clearly and distinctly, and each of the students felt as if she were speaking to him alone. Nurture your knowledge, expand your intellect – because they are free of emotion, they are merely knowledge, and there is no pain in knowledge. The pain lurks in one's thoughts, lies in wait for signs of weakness, colludes with memories. Cleanse your thoughts and you will rid yourselves of pain.

She taught them how to sit for hours, watching the greenish water of the canal. Following its slow motion. Being aware of the water and experiencing it down to the smallest ripple. She taught them to focus on the water alone, without criticism, without emotion, without judging. Just connecting with knowing the water. And then, for a short while – she said – you'll be able to let go of your thoughts. That is when you will pass through a heavy gate to the abode of pure knowledge – knowledge free of emotion, censure, suffering, pain – and you shall feel relief. They – her obedient students – would sit along the canal like beads on a huge chain, keeping a steady distance from each other so as to avoid inadvertent contact, looking at the water flowing in the canal and watching their own white garb reflected in the water, until it all seemed like one huge water snake.

She sat behind them, looked up and felt their tranquility. Like them, she let go of thoughts, relaxed her grip, erased any memory and emotion, and found solace in a pure internal awareness.

Whenever she met her students again, be it a day later or many years later, she always saw in them that ray of light that entered their soul and continued to live there like it did in her own soul. They all belonged to the Xie family, like most of the village people who had the same surname. Nanshe had been built, as family lore says, by a few families during the Song dynasty, some four hundred years ago. When Kublai Khan, the great general, invaded the Yellow River with his troops, masses of inhabitants of the central plains fled south, together with residents of the Nan kingdom, until they reached Nanshe. Over the years the founding families became a small tribe, the Xie tribe with Nanshe as its kingdom.

We've become blood-brothers, Yumin used to explain to her; a village that's a family. The people of Nanshe have always been explorers of knowledge and wisdom. That's why you feel at home here. Everyone respects both your silence and your words. We have learned that there's no need to say much. We don't even bother interpreting dreams.

That evening, when they sat on the balcony overlooking the village center, Yumin placed in her hand a statuette he had carved out of a piece of black wood he found in the river: a small figurine of a wild boar. She looked at his handiwork, at the tiny details. She understood his gaze, the way he looked at her when putting it in her hand. The wild boar was a symbol of abundance, an ancient symbol of all forms of desire. She smiled. She knew this was his way of demonstrating his feelings for her.

For years they stuck together, continually studying the foundations of the ancient beliefs. Unlike the rest of their friends, who limited themselves to studying either from writings or from teachers in the community or universities, they traveled frequently, reaching as far as the mountains kissing the skies and the kingdom of Nepal. They explored in order to find answers to their doubts. To find serenity. Sometimes it was a brief journey, a few days' foray into the capital. Other times it was a journey of months, in search of the unknown. Often the unknown would be found in a quiet cranny in the mountains, or in an isolated monastery, or an unexpected conversation with a wayfarer encountered in the expanses of the great Eastern Plains. Once their curiosity was satisfied, they began to miss their home, and would turn around and find the quickest way to get back to Nanshe.

At times they felt as if they were two strings perfectly attuned to each other in one instrument, each sensitive to the other, sharing the same vibrations. At other times they felt that the melody had stopped and that a string was about to snap. Then they would retire each to their own world, own peaceful corner. He would walk down to the tea bushes, or go on a fishing trip with his friends, and *she would go for a solitary walk in the fields, or curl up in her bed, resting and restoring, until the storm passed.*

The sun went down. The last red hues of the houses along the canal gradually turned purple, and then black. It was nighttime in Nanshe. With a smile on her face and the wild-boar figurine in her hand she sat down beside him, looking at his closed eyes, trying to penetrate his thoughts, listening to the song of the crickets that filled the darkness of the night. She stroked his face, her fingers gently combing his beard, like butterflies floating among the blades of grass, then softly kissed his eyes. When he awoke, he saw her smiling face, heard the beating of her heart, and knew she came to him for love.

He loved her tenderly. He stroked her body as if strumming the strings of her soul, sensitive to the most delicate of sounds. The melody intensified but he controlled his desire and continued to play serenely. He listened to her gentle breathing, watched her misty eyes and felt the increasing convulsions of her body, happy to know her, to discover her each time anew.

When she fell asleep, back in her own world, hugging the pillow with both hands, he picked up the boar statuette from the floor and put it next to her head.

I woke up in Haifa, with the dream still reverberating in my head. I emerged from my room and headed for the bathroom, throwing a quick "good morning" to Malca, whom I caught from the corner of my eye, then hurried into the shower, surrendering my body to the strong, hot stream, rinsing off with cold water until my hair stood on end and skin was covered in goosebumps. The cold water washed away the remains of the night and made room for adventures of the new day. I put on a light summer dress and went out to Malca.

Having morning coffee with Mandelbrot cookies on the shaded balcony, on a bright, sunny day, seemed like the beginning of a perfect holiday. Just being able to wake up naturally, without planning or setting an alarm, plus the knowledge that no patients were awaiting me, enhanced my feeling of being truly on vacation, truly free. Malca soon joined me on the porch. "Your relationship with Nathan seems serious. I understand you're meeting him today, too." When I didn't answer, she went on: "He's a good-looking man, and Junio likes him very much." Though I was glad to hear it, I felt disconcerted as usual and just smiled and thanked her. I didn't want to develop the subject. As usual, I was particular about my privacy. But I did fill her in about my plans. "We agreed to meet this afternoon, once he's through with his meetings with Steimatzky. I don't know what his plans are for the rest of the day, but as for me, I must present myself tomorrow at the District Bureau of Health, as I was instructed at the port, after disembarking. So we'll probably go there together tomorrow. Also, I wish to meet Dr. Rudolf Mayer, the owner of Molada maternity hospital on the Carmel. A colleague asked me to pass on his regards. While I'm at it, I'll try to inquire whether they have a vacancy for a physician with my qualifications and experience... Who knows, maybe they can offer me a job."

I asked Malca if she didn't find it odd that Heidi didn't cook. "We lived in one of their apartments for about four months," said Malca, and noticing my puzzlement went on to elaborate. "Herman offered Junio this living arrangement as payment for building the house. I wouldn't hear of it because I knew what would be expected of me, and refused to become the maid of a woman who can't cook or clean her own house. Herman is a nice person, generous and considerate. But Heidi looks down on everyone else. Some days they order food from restaurants, and the rest of the time a cook comes in. The cleaning is done by Yusra, a Christian Arab woman." I was surprised by this information, and understood how she felt when she continued: "Herman loves Polish food – pierogi, knishes, kugel, stuffed neck and spleen. They all require a lot of work, and I was not going to lose my freedom and become the cook for two families, especially not for a woman who doesn't lift a finger."

All this was far beyond anything I was used to in Chortkow. True, the well-off families did employ Polish and Ukrainian cooks and maids, but it was nonetheless up to the *baleboste*, the mistress of the house, to be in charge of the tidiness, cleaning and cooking. That's how it was in our own home and in Malca's home. Malca's mother, Fradel, was well known in Chortkow not only for running the family business and being an astute merchant, but also as a model housewife, famous for the best spelt knishes in the neighborhood. I completely identified with Malca, and was outraged by the thought that Junio did not immediately protect her from being exploited and was willing to even consider Herman's offer. I shared with Malca my uneasiness about Heidi and Herman's hospitality: "True, they welcomed me and Nathan and didn't bother us with too many questions, but still, I didn't feel at ease there. Something about the heavy furniture and those crystal chandeliers, perhaps. Or maybe Heidi's depressing passivity… she hardly spoke during the entire visit. Something about that house was not very pleasant. I can easily relate and understand why you wouldn't want to live in such proximity to them. I think they're the "oldest" young couple I've ever met. Yes, there definitely was something depressing about their home."

I helped Malca clean the house. The terrazzo tiles, so different from the parquet floors in Chortkow, were easy to wash and gave the house an Italian look. We aired out the bed linen, cleaned up the kitchen, and within a short while were sitting on the balcony again with a glass of cold lemonade with ice-cubes.

I asked Malca about her plans for the future – did she want to continue her studies, or get a job? She wasn't a spoiled girl; she had helped her parents in their shop and helped take care of her two younger brothers in Chortkow. "No, I want to have children of my own and bring them up," said Malca. "Junio said there's no need for me to get a job, and they don't need any help in the office. He prefers that I stay home once we have kids, and until then he prefers that the house be kept clean and neat, and that there's always food when he comes home after a long day's work. That's fine by me, even though it doesn't leave me much free time. We have neither a cleaning-woman nor a cook. I do the food shopping in the center of town, then walk uphill, carrying the shopping, all the way home. When I do have some time to spare, I prefer sitting with friends in a café and chatting. Actually, the thing I miss most is company, especially since most of my girlfriends remained in Chortkow." I watched her as she spoke, feeling the loneliness in her expression and in her voice. I was convinced that the huge change she was undergoing, from life in a large, rich family to this way of life that involved many hours of loneliness, would adversely affect her, and might even take a mental toll. But I kept those thoughts to myself.

Walking down Balfour Street was pleasant, thanks to the cool wind blowing up the mountain and through the fabric of my dress. Being already familiar with the way, I let my mind wander. I noticed that I'd passed the intersection with Herzl Street and was just opposite the Clock Tower. Only the other day, on our way to Herman's and Heidi's, Nathan had told me that this was a new office building, which was still under construction. At the top of the building there was a large clock which, strangely enough, had no numbers on its face. I assumed that was the latest style – a wall clock with no numbers on a building with no decorations. "I'm not sure I like this style," I'd said to Nathan; "If the entire city is to be built like this, it will end up quite boring. Just a collection of straight lines, bent metal pipes and polished stone, the entire city will seem like a collection of warehouses or one big industrial area."

The reception clerk greeted me with a big smile. "Hello, Madam Doctor Finkelman. Mr. Hoffman asked me to tell you that he's being delayed and will get here in about half an hour. You can either get a key for the room, or go up to the roof bar to enjoy the view, the fresh air and a drink. I'll send Mr. Hoffman right up to you when he arrives."

I sat on the roof, in the shade, opposite Mount Carmel, and ordered a cup of tea. In the center of the tiled roof there was a bar, with tables and chairs around it. Two British officers were having a lively conversation at one end, and a small group of women sat nearby, talking in German. I smiled to myself as it suddenly dawned on me that Haifa was becoming quite a cosmopolitan city. The immigrants from Central Europe, the government administrators and British soldiers, and the local Arab residents all created a new world. A world characterized by a mixture of spoken languages and an assortment of architectural styles. It was all, without a doubt, different from anything I'd encountered in Europe.

I jumped up, startled, when I felt a hand on my shoulder. Nathan surprised me. I didn't hear him approach, engrossed as I was in my thoughts that wandered back and forth between Chortkow and Haifa.

"The doctor is enjoying herself, soaking up the sun?" He addressed me jovially in third person, the polite Polish way. I could feel myself melting under his gaze, his penetrating look making me blush, or perhaps it was just the sun's heat. The German women at the other end of the roof stared at us, sizing us up, as if trying to decipher the meaning of this rendezvous on the roof.

Had these ladies been able to see through the floor of the roof into the room where we made love, they'd correctly conclude that this was a rendezvous of desire that reached its fulfilment.

Honestly – I'd never experienced such a feeling before. Who knows – maybe it was the meeting in a hotel, accompanied by associations of wantonness typical of schund – pulp fiction – that ignited my passion. Or maybe it was the total freedom from any obligations to work and family which gave rise to emotions I wasn't familiar with.

The gushing storm abated, I lay in Nathan's arms, hypnotically watching the ceiling fan turn slowly, wishing that this moment would never end.

We dozed off for a while, and when we awoke I told Nathan about my dreams. As I was relating them I got increasingly curious to figure out their meaning. We discussed it and decided that the character in my dreams was probably me. The other details of the dreams were very strange, definitely not part of my world. I shared this thought – my feeling that it was as if I'd become part of a different world – with Nathan. Obviously, the dream symbolized something that was of importance to me, but I couldn't work out what it was, and Nathan couldn't help me. For a moment I thought that the characters in the dream spoke Chinese, or Japanese – that's what I seemed to remember. And strangely enough, I'd understood them. When I said so to Nathan, he replied immediately: "Dreams have a logic of their own, which cannot always be followed. Your need to find the underlying logic in everything is obsessive. Learn to let go, there's no reason for you to trouble yourself, especially when it comes to things of obscure meaning." I smiled to myself: That's precisely what I was – obsessive.

We decided to stay in bed. We ordered a light meal from room service, and felt happy and disconnected from the outside world. Even the strange dreams and my frustration over my inability to decipher them stopped bothering me.

The following day was very busy. It began with showing up at the State Bureau of Health, as I'd committed to do at

Border Control in Haifa Port. After a prolonged wait, I met with a nurse-clerk or clerk-nurse who inquired about my health then signed and stamped my form without waiting for my answer that I was well.

From there I hurried to my meeting with Dr. Rudolf Mayer at Molada maternity hospital. Nathan joined me, and we took a taxi up the mountain. The small maternity hospital was at the top of Mount Carmel, ideally located for a perfect view of Haifa Bay.

As great as my excitement was over the beautiful view, so was my disappointment with the maternity hospital. The building seemed better suited to be a hotel than a maternity hospital, or any modern hospital meant to serve a growing city. At best, it looked like a private clinic that provided birthing assistance as well as basic medical procedures, and some simple surgeries, mostly of the gynecological type. The location of the hospital was also odd, in my opinion. My understanding was that a maternity hospital ought to be located in the community, not secluded on top of a mountain without easy transportation. Once again, despite my natural tendency, I forced myself to refrain from expressing myself aloud.

At the end of our tour of the hospital, Dr. Meir asked for my Haifa address so that he'd be able to contact me should they need additional medical staff. That was his polite way of telling me that they did not need more physicians.

We left on foot, walked down to the center of town, and looked for a café.

***

Khayat Beach

I never imagined that bathing in the sea could be such an erotic experience. Maybe erotic isn't quite the right word to describe my feeling, but I couldn't find the word that would more accurately describe my reactions when I first walked into the water of the Mediterranean.

I love to swim. In a film taken of me as a child, you can see my father carrying me on his back in the river that crosses Chortkow. Later, I enjoyed going swimming in lakes and rivers. But the Mediterranean was an entirely different matter; its water was so clear, and the warmth of the water was a pleasant surprise. The clear water entered every hidden corner of my body.

I lay on my back, easily floating on the briny sea. It was so different. I didn't have to struggle in order to stay afloat, as if gravity didn't apply to this body of water. Though, of course, I was aware that it was the salt water that was enabling me to float with ease, shut my eyes and soak up the caressing rays of the sun.

Nathan's hands did the rest.

I'd never before swum in such clear water. Even the ripples didn't disturb its clarity. I could see schools of tiny fish crazily zigzagging in the water. Every once in a while a few fish jumped out of the water, their bodies sparkling like silver ribbons in the sun. Until that morning, the bathtub at home and in the mikveh, the ritual bathhouse, were the only places I'd ever seen clear water. The water seen in that film taken in my childhood, as well as the water in the stream where I learned to swim, was greenish, and the bottom of the stream was muddy. The seawater at Khayat Beach, in contrast, was like crystal, and the bottom of the sea where my feet were standing was sandy, yellowish, as if made of grains of gold.

We swam quite a way. I felt total freedom. Mount Carmel jutted against the backdrop of the beach while, opposite it, the sea extended and joined the blue sky somewhere in the horizon. Never in my life had I experienced such a sensation of total freedom as I did in those clear blue waters opposite the Carmel.

***

Ethel

As a child, I loved and admired my sister Ethel. She was the only one in our family who could deal with Mother's complete control. We all called her Ethel or Ethelka, even though Father wanted her name to be Leah, and that's how she was registered at birth. Father had a weakness for Biblical and Aramaic names, which was why he chose the name Leah, which means lady in ancient Acadian. Years later, when she was living in the United States, Ethel wrote to me that, apparently, in Old English the name Ethel means a noble woman.

Ethel gave birth to Fabiush when she was twenty three; I was fourteen at the time. He was my parents' first grandchild, but instead of happiness his birth brought them only pain and shame. Chortkow was not used to children being born out of wedlock, and in our own family it was considered an absolute disaster.

To this day I don't know why Ethel and Abraham, or Arnold as he preferred being called, didn't marry. When Arnold left for the States I was too young, and later Mother refused to talk about it. He was different from the rest of us. Word in the family was that his mother was Italian and that there was doubt about her Jewishness. But Ethel insisted that she came from the nearby town of Zolotyi Potik. Rumors also said that his father was of Russian origin, but no one could say when and how his family came to Chortkow. If the rumors were true, then marriage would have been out of the question. Arnold was an architect, a year older than Ethel. I remember him as tall, thin, with coal-black hair. They said that he'd studied architecture in Vienna, and when he came back from his studies he won over Ethel's heart and broke our parents'.

At first, the couple moved into a small apartment by the river, close to the timber warehouse of Uncle Eliyahu, Father's younger brother. But as time passed and Ethel's pregnancy became more noticeable, she preferred to spend her time at our place, especially on days when Arnold was away on business. Mother learned to quit criticizing her, Ethel learned not to respond to every comment, while I was happy I could ask for her help with my homework, and share stories and gossip from school.

Ethel went back to work for Father. No one could manage the books and keep track of the stock of wood as expertly as Ethel did. Father never bothered her with comments or unwanted questions, nor did he reproach her when she first told him about their plan to move to the United States. I even heard him defending the idea once when talking with Mother: "Arnold has a profession, he'll find work. This is a good opportunity for Ethel to leave Chortkow and start a new life, free of prejudice." Father's support of Ethel was a rare event. Usually, he preferred not to pick a fight with Mother, not to disagree with her nor to express his own opinions concerning Ethel. In fact, I suspect the move sounded like a good idea to Mother – an excellent way to keep the shame away from the family.

The person whom Ethel really missed during her ordeal was our sister Zelda – her only ally in the family. Together, they were a joint force that could deal with Mother. Zelda, a year younger than Ethel, was studying philosophy in Lwow and was close to finishing her PhD thesis. She was good at talking and arguing, as philosophers often are, and she knew how – though it was by no means easy – to change Mother's firm opinions.

Fabiush was born on a freezing cold morning. The midwife arrived quickly, despite the layer of ice covering Chortkow. I remember clearly Ethel's screaming and cursing everyone within earshot. Most of all, she cursed Arnold who, as usual, was away on business out of town, and was not present at the birth. At the end of all the grunting, groaning and wailing, Fabiush's cry was heard, as if announcing "Here I am!"

Looking back on those days, I think this period may have been the quietest and perhaps the happiest period of Ethel's life. But maybe I should rephrase: it may not have been the calmest and happiest time, but it was rich in optimism.

Baby Fabiush's brit was unusual in many respects. Since it was Father's first grandson, it should have been a big occasion; then again – a child out of wedlock is not the sort of thing to brag about. The compromise was a brit ceremony held at home, with family, a few close friends, and a few of father's colleagues from nearby towns.

After the brit things did not calm down at home. Ethel, Arnold and little Fabiush moved to the apartment next-door, the main entrance to which was from the adjacent Szpitalna Street, meaning "Hospital Street". It was explained to me that Mother wanted to be able to help Ethel, especially when Arnold was away in Lwow. The way I saw it, Father simply wanted Ethel to continue to manage his accounts. So everyone benefited from this arrangement.

Little Fabiush had strong, healthy lungs and a very loud cry. He turned night into day and day into night, which became the family's new routine. One day, Mother and Ethel announced that in the afternoons, after school and after homework, it would be my turn to help take care of Fabiush, so that they could do their chores, as well as take a short nap, as I was to discover. I liked being with Fabiush. He was amusing, didn't cry much when I was with him, and laughed when I made faces at him. I learned how to feed him from a bottle and change his diapers. He became a kind of attraction for my girlfriends who would come to visit us and have fun with him.

Arnold left home for the States less than a year after Fabiush was born. He followed in the footsteps of his father, Haim Zelig, who'd immigrated to New York about a year earlier, before the birth of his first grandchild. The plan was for Arnold to join his father. He hoped that his education and professional experience as an architect and civil engineer would enable him to receive an immigration permit and find work in New York. Ethel and Fabiush were supposed to join him later and embark on a new life. But – as Father used to say in Yiddish – "*Mann tracht, un Gott lacht*" – Man plans and God laughs. The Great War broke out, Ethel and Fabiush were in a city that was being bombed, whereas Arnold was at the other end of the world, in New York.

During the war we were under Russian rule for almost three years and, towards the end of the war, also under the Bolsheviks. We all suffered deprivation. Early on, the war brought a deluge of immigrants that flooded the area. Most of them came from the east, from the direction of Russia, and a smaller number came from the south. Most Jews lost their livelihoods and many contracted one of the rampant plagues: smallpox, dysentery, typhoid fever, and cholera. About a third of Chortkow's population perished. Mother says that that was when I first started expressing my wish to become a doctor, "because it's unacceptable that people should just die like flies."

During the war there was no communication between Ethel and Arnold – a total break. It was very rare for any letters to reach Chortkow; a few arrived from relatives in other countries, some had even contained cash that was often stolen en route. But Ethel didn't receive any sign of life, and Arnold's name was nearly forgotten in our home. Once the war ended, the fighting over control of Galicia began between Ukraine, Austria, Russia and Poland, until in 1918 the Second Republic of Poland assumed de facto control over west Galicia. That was when the first letter arrived. I was at home looking after the two boys when Father and Ethel came back from the train station. It was the first time in months that a load of wood had arrived. Their expressions made it clear that something was up. Ethel's eyes were red from crying and Father was restless, waiting for Mother to come in. Fabiush felt the tension, and dashed outside with Junio, away from the danger zone, as it were. Only when Mother came in did I first notice the envelope in Ethel's hand: the first letter from Arnold after four years. Reading the letter made it clear that it was preceded by dozens of earlier letters that had never made it to their destination, probably lost in the turmoil of war. Arnold wrote about his life in America, about his work as a civil engineer, which, over the years, took him to different locations, including in New York, and even Mexico a few times. He wrote that, at present, he was living with his father in an apartment at 272 East 4th street in south Manhattan, and asked Ethel to come and join him.

Two more years passed until Ethel and Fabiush embarked on their journey to unite with Arnold in the U.S. By that time I was no longer at home; I'd moved to Lwow and started studying medicine. For a long time, until the day she departed, Ethel tried to persuade me to quit my studies, come with her and study medicine in New York. We both knew this was not a realistic prospect. Not only because our family couldn't possibly afford the huge expense involved, considering the hard times in Chortkow following the war, but especially because my limited knowledge of English was far from the level required for academic studies. What's more, I was the first Chortkow woman to be accepted to Medical School in Lwow, and I was not going to risk it for the sake of some vague dream.

After that first letter, the correspondence between Chortkow and New York became regular. Once a month Ethel would get a letter, retire to her room, and the following morning would hurry to the post office to send her reply. She attached photos of Fabiush and herself, and received from Arnold photos of him and of the house that was to be her new home. Days went by. Months passed. Arnold was waiting for immigration papers for his family, and Father was saving money for the voyage and putting it aside together with the money Arnold was sending to me.

At last, in the middle of June 1920 Ethel and Fabiush set out on their long journey, which began on trains across Europe: from Chortkow in east Poland, via Warsaw and Berlin, to Copenhagen, Denmark. They set sail from Christiania Port on June 6th, aboard the Hellig Olav, and after sixteen days, on June 22nd, reached their destination and reunited with Arnold.

The Hellig Olav, 1920

Ethel's first letter from NYC arrived on August 4th, 1920. She'd addressed it to my small apartment in Lwow, which I moved to after having finished my first year of studies. "We crossed Europe, crossed the huge ocean, and finally met Arnold," she wrote. "It was an exhausting journey. To my surprise, the sea voyage was the easy part. The difficult part was the train journey. We had to spend a few days in

Lublin, Warsaw and Berlin. Fabiush was not the ideal travel companion… He was impatient and felt very ill-at-ease in the big cities. Maybe he was excited, or nervous, at the prospect of the sea voyage, or of meeting his father whom he didn't know. I was excited, too. And apprehensive: I wasn't sure what kind of Arnold I would meet.

"Time had been kind to Arnold. American-style clothing suited him. A mischievous, restless glimmer in his eyes gave him away. Under the new appearance, it was the same Arnold that I loved."

The letter was full of details about Ethel's first week in New York. She was amazed at the sight of the huge, tall buildings, the wide streets and the pace of everyday life in the big city. She joked at the fact that there were parts of the city where you could get along fine with Yiddish; you didn't have to speak English. But she did enroll for English classes, and did the same for Fabiush, in addition to his attending a Jewish school in the southeast of Manhattan.

What was missing from this and the following letters were words expressing emotion – the emotions of a woman who has finally reunited with her loved one after so many years. The letters were full of information about Arnold's work and Fabiush's schooling. She also mentioned that her English was not good enough for her to work in accounting, and she has had to learn to sew so as to help support the family.

I missed the heart-to-heart talks we used to have in the past. I suspected she made an effort to write neutral letters that would pass unscathed under Mother's inquisitive eyes and would answer other family members' curiosity.

Only when she wrote to me alone, at my Lwow address, did she pour her heart out. That's when she wrote to me about the day-to-day difficulties of life with Arnold. She wrote about the cultural gap between them, and about his inability to find peace and quiet, a restlessness that drove her crazy. She wrote about their trip to Mexico for his work, and her anger at having to uproot Fabiush once again, after he had succeeded in adapting to his new environment, despite the difficulties. But she did also enjoy some relief when, at long last, they succeeded in sorting out their marriage license, having reported to the local authorities that the original marriage registration papers were lost during the Bolshevik revolution.

Ethel's letters continued to arrive on a monthly basis, and when I graduated and returned to Chortkow, I also received a small parcel with a beautiful Ford Bell, British stethoscope. The card said: "To my beloved sister, the first Finkelman woman to become a Doctor and the first in Chortkow – hope this wonderful tool will help you also listen to and understand your heart's desires."

I sent my reply straightaway: "The stethoscope is beautiful, and of a kind that can't be acquired around here. But even this wondrous and sensitive tool will not be able to read my heart. I've been facing great challenges. Establishing a clinic in Chortkow and the difficulty of getting patients has been using up all my energy, leaving nothing for matters of the heart. Or maybe that's just an excuse, and the truth is that the men I love are always either married or spoken for, so it seems like I'll be using the stethoscope for medical purposes only for the foreseeable future."

I was surprised when Ethel wrote that they'd moved to Los Angeles. There was something restless in these shifts from country to country, which seemed to me to point to disquiet or adaptability issues. I couldn't understand how Fabiush handled such frequent changes. Arnold opened his own architecture firm in Los Angeles, and their financial situation improved immensely, thanks to a surge in construction in the city. Ethel said that most of Arnold's work was in the center of the city, and that most of his clients were from the Jewish community, including producers, directors, actors and movie studio managers. She wrote about the houses and villas he'd designed, and even a synagogue called Beit Yisrael on Sunset Boulevard in Hollywood, the home of film-making.

Years went by. Arnold's letters continued to describe his impressive achievements. Junio, who was home on vacation from his architecture studies in Vienna, served as the family's interpreter, helping us to understand the significance of Arnold's achievements.

The crowning glory of Arnold's architectural achievements was a large housing project in a new part of Hollywood. The impressive project, named Chateau Marmont after the street it was built on, was modeled after chateaus in the Loire Valley in France.

Drawing of the Chateau Marmont, Sunset Blvd corner of Marmont Lane, Hollywood

But hand-in-hand with Arnold's success came Ethel's tragedy. Her letters stopped, and four long months passed without a single sign of life. Then came a long letter, which concealed more than it told. The bottom line was clear enough: Ethel returned to New York on her own, without Arnold and without her son. Arnold preferred a younger woman, named Berta, who had probably brought with her, as a dowry, the Chateau Marmont project. Bertha was the sister of Fred Horowitz, a well-to-do attorney, the land owner and initiator of the project.

I never learned any further details about that tragedy. Ethel wouldn't answer my questions and later wrote that she refuses to discuss anything to do with Arnold and the break from Fabiush. She even threatened that if I continued pestering her with questions, she would stop writing altogether.

With Mother's approval, Father wrote to Ethel and offered

to pay for her to come back home. Ethel's response was laconic: "There's nothing for me in Chortkow and I don't need your pity."

I know that, since Father's business was doing better, he sent her an envelope with money each month. He never mentioned it to anyone and neither did Ethel. I learned of this from the post office manager, whose children were among my patients.

Ethel's letters became less frequent, and in 1933, after Father's death from a heart attack, they nearly stopped completely. With her typical lack of empathy, Mother used to say repeatedly: "Ethel broke Father's heart." There had never been any love lost between Mother and Ethel; Ethel was Daddy's girl. Mother couldn't accept Ethel's life story, blamed her for her own fate and referred to her as "the black sheep of the family".

This was Ethel's story, as I told it to Nathan while we lay on the warm sand on Khayat Beach, Haifa.

***

Jerusalem

Jerusalem will always have a special place in my heart.

I was in love with Nathan, and I believe that, at the time, Nathan was in love with me. One Friday morning, without my knowledge, he left the Zion hotel where he'd been staying, went over to Heidi and Herman's and rented from them the front-facing apartment on the top floor. From there he went on to the central post office and sent a telegram to the Culture League publishing house in Warsaw:

"Dear Mr. Nachman Mayzel,

I shall be finishing my work in Palestine within two weeks at the most. I wish to inform you that I have decided to remain in Haifa for the time being. I shall be happy to be at your service as necessary. My address is: 6, Nordau Street, Haifa. Attached please find a letter containing a summary of my business meetings and the ensuing agreements signed in Haifa, Tel Aviv and Beirut.

Sincerely,

Nathan Hoffman"

As it turned out, only Junio was in the know. He had served as mediator between the Heidi-Herman greed and Nathan's ability to pay for the apartment. Apparently, all this took place upon Nathan's return from Beirut, again – without my knowledge. He'd spent two days in Beirut, meeting with local book distributors, and promoting a project of printing or publishing travel-guides to Lebanon and Syria. I had wanted to join him on this trip, together with Malca, but Junio claimed the trip was too dangerous. I conceded to his opinion, but was very disappointed.

Later on, I teased Nathan by saying that the surprise step of renting the apartment had been a pretty extreme reaction to a separation of only four days. True, the separation came after about three weeks of the most intensive relationship I'd ever had, but at the same time I may have been scared of the commitment which this step might introduce into my life.

That evening, for the Sabbath meal, Nathan brought a bottle of French wine. He uncorked it and poured wine for the four of us. Before saying a blessing over the wine, as was his wont, humorously rather than using the traditional version, he handed the telegram to me and asked me to read it.

While I was trying to take in the full significance of the telegram, Nathan wished them all a Shabbat Shalom and added: "I am happy to join Haifa's Polish community." Junio smiled as a confidant might, whereas Malca looked at me questioningly, attempting to figure out why I was blushing this time. In response, I passed the telegram over to her, and she responded with amazement and delight.

That night, at the hotel, snuggling close together in bed,

I took a deep breath, looked him in the eye and asked, "So what's the next step?" Nathan replied casually, as if his mind was totally elsewhere, "I believe it's a trip to Jerusalem. We haven't been there together yet." We both burst out laughing with relief. The laughter was quickly replaced by caressing, and the caressing by lovemaking.

The three of us went on this trip: Malca, Nathan and I. Junio was way too busy supervising the concrete work at a residential building he had designed. He made it clear that the job could not be postponed, due to the constant concern over possible strikes by the unionized workers.

This was my first time out of Haifa. After an incredibly long and harrowing trip we reached Jerusalem. We'd left in the early hours of the morning on a crowded bus full of people with their agricultural produce – live chickens, bags full of onions and garlic, etc., that drove for hours on the longest and most convoluted route imaginable: We left via downtown Haifa; from there through Nazareth and Jenin, then along the west slopes of Mount Shomron and the Arab towns of Tulkarem, Taibeh and Kalkilya, as far as Petach Tikva, and then on to the center of Tel Aviv – exactly as Junio had described to me the night before. If I'm not mistaken, this trip took around six hours, most of which I slept through.

Following Junio's advice, we rested briefly, then took a different bus to Jerusalem. We left from a new station, in an area with new-looking houses, most of them of modern European style. I think the name of the street was Rothschild Boulevard, after the well-known Zionist philanthropist who funded many projects in Palestine. The drive from Tel Aviv to Jerusalem was very slow, and took about four hours; the loaded bus had a tough time coping with the winding, uphill road. Luckily for us, it was a cool day. I hate to imagine what it could have been like on a hot summer day. Even in cool weather you could smell the passengers' body odor – some of whom were in dire need of a good wash. Yes, I was sure that this same trip, in the heat of summer, would be hell.

Malca and I sat next to each other, and behind us Nathan sat next to a Middle-Eastern looking man from Jerusalem who, to our great surprise, spoke fluent German. Nathan was thrilled and the two carried on a lively conversation throughout most of the trip. This man, Simon, later helped us find our way in Jerusalem, and even accompanied us all the way to the Tel Aviv hotel on Jaffa Street, not far from the stop where the bus let us off. The hotel was also close to Jerusalem's walled-in Old City.

Malca and I shared a room; Nathan was in the next room. The rooms were spacious and had ensuite bathrooms. We took a quick shower then went out and sat in the garden of Café Vienna next to the hotel. We were familiar with the name of the café because there was one just like it on Nordau Street in Haifa, not far from Heidi and Herman's. It was like enjoying a touch of Europe in Jerusalem: three cups of coffee, apple strudel with whipped cream, sitting outdoors in cold weather, feeling as if we're at home in Europe, not here in the Levant. But the moment we raised our heads and looked around, the world took on a different appearance. Middle-Eastern Jews, who look much like the local Arabs except for their clothes and the kippah on their heads, walked by. British soldiers and officers strolled in groups, and some of them sat down at nearby tables; they obviously preferred beer with some unfamiliar snack to Viennese coffee, ice cream, or cake with whipped cream.

The encounter with the beauty of Old Jerusalem within the city walls was unforgettable, a new experience, something I'd never seen before: Ancient, awe-inspiring walls; winding lanes, old houses, colorful markets from which a dizzying mixture of strong aromas wafted our way, stinging the nose and throat, smells of spices, incense, and donkey dong. In our eminently European garb, we probably made a strange addition to the scene: A European man dressed in a dark suit and long wool coat, and two elegant-looking women dressed in the best of European fashion; all three striding energetically down the narrow lanes, adroitly avoiding dog mess and donkey dung.

We were easy prey for the market merchants pushing their wares: silk scarves that "only last night arrived from the markets of Damascus"; old Roman or Crusader coins – probably adeptly produced in a nearby metal workshop; and plenty of new and old religious items made of hammered copper or carved from olive wood, suitable for all three religions. We decided to buy a few souvenirs and gifts for friends in Chortkow, and asked Nathan to do the negotiating for us. Nathan bargained with the Arab salesmen like any experienced dealer, and managed to get us a good deal. We continued happily on our way, exploring the Old City, until sundown.

When we returned to the hotel, tired but pleased, we were welcomed by Mr. Warshawski, the hotel proprietor. He treated us to a glass of select wine and kept us company, while telling us his family history. His father used to be the Muhtar of the Ashkenazi Jewish community in Jerusalem. He was appointed by the Ottoman rulers in the early 20th century – a respected title with many advantages. Among his responsibilities were arbitrating minor conflicts within the community, and representing the community before the Turkish Sultan. Mr. Warshawski did not hide the fact that he had benefitted from this position no less than the community did.

When we felt that we were sated with alcohol and with information about the Warshawski family, we apologized and retired to our bedrooms. As soon as Malca fell asleep, I tip-toed into Nathan's room, fell into his arms and clung passionately to his body.

We were cuddled like spoons, or as Zelda used to say in Yiddish, *In puzitsieh fon spoonz,* when I asked Nathan how he got into the book business. Battling sleep, I listened to his story:

"Actually, for most of my life I wanted to be a writer, then a poet, then a writer, and so on. I managed to put letters together into words and words into sentences, but I wasn't very good at infusing them with significant content and weaving them into a good yarn. I was highly skeptical as to my abilities and remained a hobbyist writer – you know, just keeping my writing filed in a folder… Eventually I lost confidence in myself, and finally gave up on my desire to become a writer.

"But I always loved reading; I am a bookworm, and got over

my frustration by handling other people's creative writing. This led me to work for the best publishers; the Culture League enabled me to find solace in helping the greatest Yiddish writers publish their work. I became the assistant of Nachman Mayzel, the director of the publishing house. I helped him write in Yiddish for the Yiddish weekly Literary Papers. The highlight of my achievements was Mayzel's book "Bialik, his Life and his Work". It meant a lot to me – it was like touching the greatest poet of our generation. Through this project I made good connections with the Grashen Bibliatek – something like "the Penny Library", and it was they who financed my trip to Palestine.

"I was born in 1895 in the town of Gilwice, near Katowice; the eldest of many siblings. Our family had a brewery and a license for distilling alcohol and brandy. Father always walked around in a haze of alcohol. I don't think he was a heavy drinker, but the smell stuck to him. I could always smell Father before actually seeing him.

"I was sent to school in neighboring Katowice to study at Talmud Torah, a Jewish elementary school. I studied history, Hebrew literature, the Old Testament, prayers and Jewish law, as well as some Mishna and Talmud. During that time I discovered the beauty of Hebrew poetry and literature, which was so different from the Hebrew of religious texts alone.

At age seventeen I left Gilwice, much to my parents' dismay. It triggered a serious crisis. I simply refused to follow in my father's footsteps, to spend my life distilling alcohol and producing Vodka and Brandy. I wanted to become a poet. My family thought I'd lost my mind.

"I chose to study philosophy and classical studies in Kiev. Maybe that choice was my way of moving as far away from my parents as I could. I lived in Kiev for three years, then continued to Warsaw – the heart of Hebrew culture in Poland.

"I tried my hand at writing, but pretty fast understood that I did not have the talent and the emotional impetus necessary to get the creative wheels turning. For months I felt lost and went through another crisis. I worked at various casual jobs and had almost given up on ever having anything to do with the world of Hebrew poetry and literature.

That's when a chance encounter with Nachman Mayzel at a café in Warsaw changed my life. I was sitting there on my own one afternoon, reading an educational literary anthology, Lashon VaSefer, edited by Jacob Fichman, published by a respected Warsaw publishing house, and came across a children's poem? Etsbeoni, (Tom Thumb) by Haim Nachman Bialik. As I was reading it, enjoying its childlike innocence and beautiful rhyme and rhythm, I heard someone behind me reciting it, asking me:

"Who's knocking at my window? Come!"

I responded, reading from the book in front of me,

"A tiny boy – and that's Tom Thumb."

The stranger continued to recite and ask,

"Oh, what's your name, you little brother?

Who's your father? Who's your mother?"

I replied to the unknown stranger,

"No mother, father, nor name

Have I, and from no country came."

"Where do you come from, tiny child?" asked the stranger.

I retorted, "From going round the woods so wild."

"And do you take along some food?" he continued to ask,

and I said, "I need no food; there in the wood

The earth's all mine, to eat it up.

The dew's my drink, the rose my cup;

The grasshopper's my riding horse,

The spider's web my whip, of course;

And golden bees and silver flies

Bring to me my food supplies.

The humming-bird, my seamstress, sews

My lovely, gauzy, gaudy clothes…"

We both burst out laughing, and this is how I got my first job in Warsaw's literary world. The stranger who knew the Bialik poem by heart and recited it with me was none other than Nachman Mayzel, who proceeded to join me at my table. After a brief conversation he asked me to join the Culture League as an assistant editor, and later do the same job at the Grashen Bibliatek, the so-called Penny Library.

I highly disliked schund literature, the pulp fiction that had become increasingly popular. It dealt only with light, sensational stuff that reached a wide Jewish audience, including working-class blue-collars, yeshiva students and housewives. I considered it inferior, trashy literature. Hebrew and Yiddish literature, on the other hand, I considered good literature.

"Despite Grashen Bibliatek's pressure on me, I refused to deal with pulp fiction even during the difficult years of the recession. I loved my work and stuck to it. I saw the trip to Palestine as a business opportunity to develop a new kind of publishing for a new, developing world, without resorting to dealing with trash."

We fell asleep before I got the chance to tell Nathan that I believe there's nothing like a bit of schund to assuage one's heart in sleepless nights. Being engrossed in a love-story or a story about other people's troubles seemed to me one of the best antidotes for a lonely soul. Who knows – maybe it's all for the better that I didn't get to tell him.

At dawn I hurried back to my and Malca's room, showered, and got into bed to catch up on some sleep before the street noises woke us up.

The three of us got together at the breakfast table. Mr. Warshawski himself greeted us and showed us to a sunlit table, next to a window overlooking the street. Breakfast was wonderful, and included both European and Eastern delicacies. It was the first time I tasted halva, a sweet confectionary made of ground sesame seeds. It was much nicer than a similar sweet, made of sunflower seeds, that was common in Russia, Galicia and Poland.

Over a cup of black coffee, Mr. Warshawski helped us plan the day's outing. He spread a small map on the table and marked a circular route, which he said was a must for any visitor to Jerusalem. "If you get tired, you can always find a carriage or a taxi that'll take you back to the hotel. Just remember to bargain, so as not to be taken advantage of, as happens to tourists."

Soon we were walking again along the same route we walked the previous day, but this time we were determined to make the Western Wall our first goal.

We traipsed down Jaffa Street, walking east, facing the sun. Within a few minutes we found ourselves opposite the beautiful sight of the north-western corner of the wall of the Old City. We continued south along the wall, reaching the Tower of David and the Jaffa Gate.

Malca on the right, Syma on the left, Jerusalem 1935

We walked through the impressive Jaffa Gate, and as soon as we did we were flooded with the same aromas as yesterday, and the tingling in my nose was a sort of reminder of the line we crossed, from West to East.

Nathan pointed to the gate and told us its history: "Up to ten years ago, there was an impressive clock tower here, built by the Ottomans in 1907; one of six fancy towers built in various parts of Palestine. At the top of the tower there were four clocks: the westernmost one showed Europe time and the other three local time. The British took down the tower, claiming it was incongruous with the aesthetics of the old city walls."

Clock Tower, Jaffa Gate, Jerusalem, 1918

We wondered how come he knew all this, and Nathan explained: "I heard it all about two years ago here in Jerusalem at a social-cultural meeting that took place at the home of Zalman Schocken, owner of the publishing house, and hosted the German architect Erich Mendelsohn and the writer I.S. Agnon. Mendelsohn presented the story of the destruction of the Turkish clock tower as an example of removing a building of historical significance supposedly in order to improve aesthetics or as part of the prevailing world-view. Mendelsohn added humorously that the British must have been confused because the entire wall around the Old City is a product of Ottoman architecture, albeit from the sixteenth century, and the minaret known as the Tower of David is also an Ottoman creation, from the seventeenth century. "So perhaps they thought it, too, should be removed?" he quipped, and added that if he's lucky, maybe the buildings he was currently constructing in town might also one day become part of Jerusalem's history, unless they're destroyed for some reason or other. Mendelsohn confessed that he'd decided to purchase the old flour mill in Jerusalem probably because it reminded him of Potsdam, and added that he also decided to build his own home in Jerusalem."

I continued walking, smiling to myself, imagining how that conversation took place, probably in German; a conversation among intellectuals who'd moved from Europe to the Levant and brought their culture along to the new country.

On the corner of the street, close to the gate, stood a peddler who was selling golden-brown, fresh-out-of-the-oven bagels; their warm, tempting aroma floated in the air and attracted customers like magic. To our right the Tower of David stood tall, and in front of it a wide square that led to the narrow street that housed the market. It was the same path we walked the day before. The street seemed to have several names: David Street, Batrak Market Street, and Elwin Market. At first the names confused us, but we decided to walk east.

The narrow street was teeming with pedestrians. I've never seen such a motley crowd. A long, colorful parade of people, hurrying and shoving one another, some walking down hill and others climbing up: Greek priests wearing tall black hats of the type I'd seen in Chortkow; skinny, dark-skinned Abyssinians, scurrying along; Muslims wearing keffiyehs in red, black, and grey, fastened with a black cord. Bedouins wearing gowns, with short swords fastened to their belts; Ashkenazi and Sephardi Jews wearing kippot; Arab women dressed in dark robes, their faces masked by dark veils; people in European clothes and a small number of British officers. Every once in a while a porter carrying a heavy load of merchandise pushed his way through the crowd, aiming for one of the stalls; or a peddler leading a donkey weighed down by agricultural produce. The morning rush and crowd protected us from the tourist traps and tourist-hungry merchants.

We turned right and immediately knew we were on the right track, since most of the people around us wore kippot on their heads, held a typical tallit-bag under their arm and hung on to their prayer-book. Surprisingly, some of them wore the kind of Hassidic garb which I knew from Chortkow, only there such garb was reserved for the Sabbath and holidays. And, suddenly, there we were, facing the Western Wall.

What a disappointment. Maybe because I'd distanced myself from religion once I'd left home and gone away to the University of Lwow, or maybe it was because the Wall was located on a long, narrow street that looked like any other lane in the Old City. The Western Wall was less impressive in my eyes than the wall surrounding the Old City. I felt rather indifferent. Malca, on the other hand, stood there gaping, and then immediately began fervently reciting a prayer: "Blessed art thou, O Lord our God, King of the universe, who hast kept us in life, and hast preserved us, and enabled us to reach this season."

Nathan, standing next to us and observing us closely, noticed the dissimilarity between our reactions. Much later he told me that he found it difficult to understand my indifference.

Nonetheless, absent-mindedly I found myself asking "the Lord" to bestow peace of mind on Ethel.

We continued north, heading for the Via Dolorosa. The first stop was the Pretorium where, according to Christian tradition, Jesus was put on trial and condemned by the Roman Governor Pontius Pilate as a conspirator against the Crown. The feeling was as if we'd been transposed to a different city. We were out of the narrow lanes and on to a proper street, where one can easily walk without bumping into others. The pedestrians had also changed: a few groups of pilgrims walked slowly from one stop to the next. Each group was headed by a tour guide or a man of the cloth, some of them holding up a wooden cross, others assisting elderly pilgrims. Since we didn't know the route nor the stops along Jesus' way, we tagged along, following one of the groups. It was weird to hear some of the group members speaking Polish among themselves. We continued to follow them, keeping a respectable distance, while behind us we heard a group of Italian speaking pilgrims.

So we followed Jesus from one station of the Via Dolorosa to the next, until we reached the Church of the Holy Sepulcher, also called the Church of Resurrection, perhaps Christianity's holiest place. I couldn't refrain from comparing it to the holiest place for Jews, which is actually an old wall, part of a wall around a temple that no longer exists, in a sorely run-down street, without as much as a bench or chair next to it.

Nathan surprised us with one more strange story. He pointed to a cedar wood ladder on the second floor of the church façade, standing on a protruding ledge, with its top leaning on the wall just beneath the right window. "It's called the Immovable Ladder". Until 1831 the church would open its doors to the public only on special holidays and with the authorization of the Muslim authorities. At all other times the gates were locked and the monks were in fact locked in. According to stories, the food for the Armenian monks would be brought to the church in baskets, to the point just below the open window on the top floor. The monks would use the ladder to get through the window onto the ledge, from whence they'd pull up the basket of food with a rope. In 1831 a status-quo agreement was reached, covering the hours of prayer for each ethnic group and the order of lighting candles and oil lamps in the church. Some say that there were even further restrictions and agreements, such as on which floor-tiles were believers of certain ethnicities allowed to step on when walking from their place of prayer to the holy sepulcher. The ladder was part of the status quo agreement, and the spot allocated to it was not open to change. Even now, when the church gates are open every day of the week and the ladder is no longer in use, no one is allowed to move it, despite its being totally useless in any practical or religious sense."

I found it hard to believe that a wooden ladder had been standing there for some two hundred years, unused for the last hundred or so. Yet, if this story is true, I thought, what better example of the obstinacy and stupidity of religious institutions, typical apparently to all religions.

That evening, at dinner time in the hotel, I took the

opportunity to check the authenticity of Nathan's story with Mr. Warshawski.

Nathan was offended by my expressed doubts as to the veracity of his story, but his offence turned to a smile of victory when he heard Mr. Warshawski's answer: "As much as the story sounds far-fetched, it is totally true. Nothing exemplifies better the obstinacy of Jerusalemites of different religions. If you can imagine such obstinacy among the different branches of Christianity, just try to imagine the level of obstinacy among the different religions in this city – Muslims, Christians and Jews. There's no future for coexistence here. The strongest party calls the shots. That's why you didn't see any chairs, benches or other street furniture next to the Western Wall, for use during prayer. The Muslims object and the British impose their preferences, as any tyrant does, on his subjects. That's why this city will never know peace and quiet till the end of time. Each one is willing to live only according to his own beliefs."

I was all too familiar with animosity fed by religious belief. There had always been animosity between Ukrainians, members of the Orthodox Church and the Polish Catholics. The only thing they had in common was their hatred for the Jews. But the Jews in Chortkow weren't much better: there had always been bad blood between Hassidim and their opponents, the Mitnagdim, and between those two and the Jewish Enlightenment movement known as the Haskala. Not to mention that they all treated women as inferior and educated women with contempt. Of course there were those who respected anyone different, but they were a tiny minority who usually left for big cities or overseas.

The immovable ladder, The Holy Sepulcher, Jerusalem, 1935

Warshawski turned out to be a sensitive person who understood our gloom. He took a freezing-cold bottle out of the fridge and poured the transparent liquid into small glasses: "This is just the right time for drinking 'lions' milk', or as the locals call it 'halib el s'baeh'. It's the local version of Arak, very similar to Greek Ouzo, Turkis Raki, French Pernod and Pastis, Spanish Anisado and Italian Liqueur Sambuca. Lion's milk makes men feel like lions and turns women into lionesses."

He said a blessing over the drink and downed it in one gulp. We followed suit, coughing and going red in the face in reaction to its strength. The smell of anise filled the dining hall.

Warshawski looked me straight in the eye and said, "Doctor, surely you know that anise has a calming effect on the digestive system. And its qualities as an aphrodisiac are even more important. That's why, together with alcohol, it releases inhibitions. Many believe that Arak is the original nectar, the drink of the gods."

I felt as if ants were crawling up my legs, and immediately downed another glass to calm down the fire inside me. Alcohol and I were good friends. Vodka – Arak's less-refined relative, was the most popular drink among students of medicine, and had helped me many a time to loosen up and let go of inhibitions.

With hindsight I can say, that the Arak proved its wonderful worth as fuel for desire. We didn't even bother to hide the fact that we were going into the same bedroom, from which we emerged only the following morning.

Jerusalem will always have a special place in my heart.

***

6, Nordau

I moved in with Nathan at the Finkelman home two days after the census of Haifa's Jewish population. The census was quite an amusing event. At five o'clock in the afternoon Malca opened the front door and let in two grown men in formal suits, who introduced themselves as representatives of the Committee of Haifa's Jewish Community. They claimed their task was to register all of Haifa's Jewish residents, with their exact addresses. I claimed that I was merely in Haifa as a tourist, visiting my family, but they said it wasn't their job to check for visas but just to state the current residency of Jews in Haifa according to the residents' declarations and according to who is there, as far as they can tell. They wrote down Malca and me as present, and added Junio only after Malca provided them with his identity card showing his address: 15 Hillel Street, Haifa.

The event became even funnier when, a week later, those same census takers came knocking on Nathan's door on Nordau Street. When I opened the door, they looked at me in surprise, as if they'd seen a ghost. "Aren't you the lady from

Hillel Street who's visiting her family?" asked one of them in Polish. "Then there must be two of me," I joked, and offered them tea and cookies. And so Nathan, too, was registered as belonging to Haifa's Jewish community, even though we were both proud Polish citizens.

Getting the apartment furnished was quite easy. Heidi and Herman had some spare pieces of furniture which came in a container from Austria, and for which they had no use. The rest of the items, mostly second-hand, Junio acquired with the help of Shmuel Liebman, the carpenter, originally from Chortkow. The double bed squeaked with every move, but we considered it a love song every time we made love.

More surprising was the fact that I'd started working as a pediatrician without ever having decided that I wanted to do so. There was a surplus of doctors in Haifa, just like in other major cities in Palestine. This resulted from the huge increase in the immigration of doctors following the Nuremberg laws. In one year alone, some three hundred and sixty doctors arrived from Europe, mostly from Germany. Consequently there was a ratio of one doctor per one hundred and seventy five residents. Respective salaries went down and, as a result, some doctors even went through job retraining and changed careers in order to support their families.

I was, therefore, surprised when I found myself approached by Haifa families to treat their children. It was all the result of word of mouth, which passed on from the several dozen Chortkow people to other Polish speakers. They simply preferred their children to be treated by a doctor who spoke their language and was familiar with their culture, so I suppose that's why they put their trust in me.

I hadn't wanted to work as a doctor. I did not register in Palestine as a doctor and therefore did not get the appropriate work permit. Nonetheless, I began seeing patients. They simply came, knocked on the door and asked to come in. They came with children and babies, huffing and puffing from climbing up to the fourth floor. Sometimes they'd call Heidi and Herman's phone number, who lived on the second floor. Heidi spoke only German, so communication was only through Herman. Once the Finkelmans agreed to help, I'd give them a page every morning on which I'd written my reception hours for that day. At noon I'd knock on their door again and ask for the page with the names of the prospective patients and the time of their appointments. I worked three days a week, only in the afternoon, and saw up to four patients a day, between four and seven p.m.

The patients paid 50 Palestinian mil a visit, an amount equal to about the price of twenty eggs in the market, or half the daily pay of a laborer. It turned out that some of the patients found this fee too high. This income enabled me to contribute to our rent, without having to lower our standard of living. In addition, I served as in-house physician for Herman, Heidi, and their teenage son Yehuda – and so the price of our collaboration cost me the loss of my privacy.

Nathan, together with the Steimatzky team in Haifa, continued to develop the travel guides for Syria and Lebanon, and even had additional business trips to Beirut planned. But their project suffered a sudden-death blow; without any warning, a new travel guide book in Hebrew unexpectedly appeared on the market, called 'Lebanon – Land of Tourism and Summer Vacation'. The book was produced in Paris and published by the Economics Department of the Lebanese government. It was quite comprehensive and contained detailed information about thirty four sites. Even though the book was marred by many errors, according to Nathan, including spelling mistakes due to unprofessional editing, including the book's title – it was nonetheless a serious blow to Steimatzki's original project.

I liked the Lebanese book, especially its introduction which promoted Lebanon as an ideal place for a vacation: "Thanks to its beauty and splendor, Lebanon became a parable for poets and prophets alike. The wisest man, the writer of the Song of Songs, wanted Lebanon to be home to his beloved, Shulamite. He spent his honeymoon there, inviting his fiancée by saying "Come with me from Lebanon, my bride, come with me from Lebanon; look from the top of Amana, from the top of Senir and Hermon, from the lions' dens, from the mountains of the leopards... and the smell of thy garments is like the smell of Lebanon. "And ever since, for thousands of years, the sublime Lebanon continued to be the height of man's pride and desire."

Lebanon, land of tourism and summer vacations, 1935. (Sic! Hand-written corrections in the original)

This turned out to be a bad omen. A heavy cloud of darkness descended on Nathan. I tried to encourage him by saying that there was no need to drop the idea of publishing travel guides in Hebrew for neighboring countries, but all I elicited from him was a "You don't understand" kind of look. In fact, dropping the original initiative did not come from Nathan but from Steimatzky. They were discouraged by the unexpected competition, and Nathan didn't have much say in the matter.

Nathan had financial resources, liquid savings. I, too, had money, we would not have had difficulties in supporting ourselves together even without his work. The cost of living in Palestine was far cheaper than in Poland or Germany. I thought that Nathan would have no problem finding a decent job, because of his extensive experience in publishing, and especially considering his connections in Europe with Steimatzky and with Schocken.

But Nathan's dream, which he'd woven for weeks and following which he'd decided to remain in Haifa, had come undone. As if his hope of doing something significant suddenly disappeared into thin air. Perhaps his sense of failure became all the stronger, bringing back memories of the time when he first realized he lacked the talent to be creative in poetry or literature.

Suddenly I was living with a different Nathan. I had to respect his privacy, give him the space and quiet he required. I suppose I wasn't very good at it. In the days that followed I saw him withdraw into himself; sensitive and avoiding contact, as if on the defense. He would leave the house, go down to the street and walk around the streets of Haifa for hours. Walking alone, politely turning down any suggestion of shared activity. He made Junio his main interlocutor, in effect abandoning me.

Then the cloud lifted just as suddenly as it had descended, just like the ups and downs of spring weather. Nathan's frustration was replaced by energetic action. He initiated meetings in Haifa, Tel Aviv and Jerusalem, and searched for publication and quality printing projects in Europe.

As days went by, living together eroded romance. Maybe we were too hasty to enter into a routine with a fixed daily agenda which included work and social commitments; and maybe we lost some of our freedom through attempting to please and placate each other.

I'd never before shared a home with a man for more than one or two nights, certainly not for a long period, and at the age of thirty-seven I suppose it's hard to change one's old habits and to experience love that supersedes one's need for privacy.

I did not do laundry, neither mine nor Nathan's. I'd always hated doing laundry. I paid Yusra, Heidi and Herman's housekeeper, to do our laundry and clean the apartment, and thus protected the delicate skin of my hands. Nathan was in charge of doing the day-to-day shopping: fruit and vegetables, fish and meat, mostly from the Arab peddlers in the market. Other items such as bread, cheese, and so on were bought at the Tnuva grocery store nearby.

We carried on a multilingual life: With Heidi and Herman we spoke German; with Malca and Junio and people in the street we spoke mostly Hebrew; we made love in Polish and squabbled and cursed in Yiddish. Most of my patients spoke Polish, but with a few I spoke German or Hebrew. Many times I'd start a sentence in one language and finish it in another. I continued to dream in Polish. I thought to myself that moving from one culture to the other while maintaining old habits was quite exhausting. Most of the time I felt tired, and missed my privacy.

Nathan spoke very little about his family. Like me, he too had never married nor raised a family. He claimed he never abstained from women, but was very wary about losing his privacy, so for most of his life had dreaded the thought of sharing his home long-term with a woman.

So we found ourselves, for the first time in our lives, two adults anxious about their privacy, yet living together in one smallish apartment.

We took care not to tread on each other's toes; we tried to maintain our privacy and create a personal space for each, but this caution did not come naturally to us. I guess you can't love someone cautiously.

Thoughts of leaving everything behind and going back home to Chortkow began to pass through my mind, as if charting an escape route from the reality that had formed around me.

Later on, I thought that our love had been the spring of our lives; it had sprung and bloomed quickly, like daffodils after a long winter, then faded and dried up as soon as summer arrived.

As my sister Zelda used to say in Yiddish, "Libe kanen tsetl durkh a farmakht fentzter", meaning love can escape even through a closed window. That's what happened to my love for Nathan. One day it snuck out, escaped and never returned.

***

Third Dream

The village calm was suddenly disrupted. For a moment it seemed as if life was still going on peacefully. The sky smiled a yellow smile at dawn and reddened with the sunset. Only a sensitive, keen eye could sense the change taking place in nature. Most human beings had long since lost the ability to sense approaching disasters. But when she sat that day on her balcony, she was amazed by the huge number of birds in the sky. It wasn't the usual bird migration she'd been used to. As a child, she loved to lie on her back on the lawn around her home, enjoying the sun and counting the birds that flew across the sky. In Nanshe there were never many migrating birds, which is why she now felt as if she were observing a familiar sight from her childhood. But the clouds of birds kept increasing until they practically covered the entire sky. Then she noticed that bugs, ants, geckos and other lizards were exiting their hiding places and crawling through the village paths, all heading in the same direction, to the open fields. The silence broke down. As if responding to an unheard command, all the dogs began barking and the cats meowing restlessly and running southwards. The mayhem kept increasing and the noise of the house pets and farm animals became unbearable. She recalled a story her father told her about the monks' ability to foresee natural disasters based on the animals' behavior. But nothing else seemed to be amiss, only the animals lost their composure. The village people stood in the streets, watching the sky. Nanshe's sky had never been covered with migrating birds, so most of the local denizens attributed the animals' behavior to the appearance of the birds. Everyone knew that one bird could drive a cat crazy, so obviously a sky full of birds which were blocking the sun could do much worse. The disquiet increased once a few people reported that the water level in the canal was fluctuating. The water-line, which was stable all year round, was suddenly going up and down in an inexplicable cycle. From her spot on the balcony, she could see people grouping together, looking at the canal and at the sky, proposing explanations, while not reaching any consensus.

Her amazement grew when she noticed that the goldfish that were swimming in circles in the clay pot in the garden were helplessly trying to jump out. At first she thought they might be hungry, but when they showed indifference to the food she gave them, she realized their behavior, too, was connected to the weird phenomena all around.

Darkness began to fall. Yumin was late. Were they facing an approaching natural disaster? She wanted him next to her. She sat there, waiting anxiously. He returned along with strange lights in the sky. The moment he walked in, flames of light began striking the sky intermittently. They looked a bit like lightning, but their movement was circular, strange, a bit like the blue flashes created by a wool blanket on a dry winter day. Yumin looked concerned. "This can't be the sign of a storm or downpour because Monsoon season is about four months away," he said. An earthquake, maybe? He thought, but not aloud. But she sensed his thoughts, and said, in a questioning tone, "An earthquake is approaching."

All of a sudden the turmoil stopped. The birds fell silent and thousands of stars shone in the sky. The goldfish calmed down. A silent calm descended on Nanshe. The mayhem passed just as suddenly as it started.

He hurried to wash the dust and dirt off his body, and while still wet, brought them both cups of tea. They sipped it slowly under the night sky, savoring its excellent aroma. Their eyes focused on random points in space, and the silence respected their stillness. The cups were long empty, but still they sat, watching and giving in to the silence. Nanshe was totally dark. The last of the street-lights were off. Only the stars were reflected in the canal water.

Then all of a sudden, out of the silence, they felt a tremor. The earth roared. They felt as if they were riding on the back of a huge old dragon who'd suddenly come to life.

Everything shook, quivered, vibrated. Objects fell. The smell of dust filled the air. Shouting was heard from the street. Nanshe woke up in fright. The tremors continued for a few minutes, then froze. They stayed sitting in place, petrified with fear, breathing fast. Then they grasped that their home had survived. Nanshe survived.

They clung to each other, happy that they'd survived, as their breathing calmed down. It was more a strong grasp than an embrace, but they found encouragement and peace holding on to each other. Despite the major tremor, she understood that the origin of the quake was quite far away, and immediately understood the direction of the birds' flight – they had been distancing themselves from the epicenter of the quake. The quake originated far away to the north east. Immediately she was engulfed by concern for her family, her home town. She remembered stories she heard as a child, of huge dragons living in the center of the earth who, when disturbed, wake up angry from their sleep and shake up the whole world. The angrier they are, the worse the earthquake they cause.

Finally, the land was still, and Nanshe woke up once again to peace and quiet. Hundreds of lights lit the village like fireflies in a dark forest; first at house entrances, then in the alleys and streets. Everyone went out to check the damage. Some stood at the entrance to the temple, talking, comparing, trying to figure out the location of the epi-center of the earthquake and assess the damage. Once everyone calmed down, realizing that no significant damage had been caused, they lost interest and dispersed to their homes. The night was tranquil once again, but Nina knew, or felt, that somewhere out there, the world had suffered severely, or even been destroyed.

I woke up in fright. For a few moments I wasn't sure whether I was in Chortkow, in Haifa, or in some village in Asia, called Nanshe, about which I'd dreamt before. I took a notebook and pen out of my bag and sat down to write the dream before it evaporated. My dreams were usually few and far between, and didn't linger. They'd escape my memory incredibly fast. Only when I managed to hold on to them and write them down immediately did they see fit to stay with me forever.

I wrote down this dream as a continuation of the previous one. How strange, I thought, that such strange dreams should follow one another within such a short time. When I finished writing and re-read both dreams, I was amazed at how interwoven they were with each other.

Having studied medicine, I knew that dreams were a kind of suppressed thoughts or wishes; at least that's what Freud claimed, if I'm not mistaken, when he added an important layer to understanding the significance of dreams. I heard that sometimes dreams point to choices in one's life, or even carry prophetic significance. Some say that dreams can warn you of things that might happen. The market in Chortkow housed many fortune-tellers and dream-interpreters, but their clients were mostly peasants. Jews preferred going to their rabbis to interpret their dreams, while rich people took advantage of modern medicine and psychiatry. As for me, my view of fortune-tellers and prophetic dreams was the same – complete disbelief.

But this time was different, and actually scared me. Those dreams I had were so detailed and realistic, as if I had actually experienced them, as if they were about me. I was a doctor, and the character in the dream had also studied medicine. On the other hand, the nature of the village, its landscape, houses, vegetation, animals and people, were nothing like my real world. Though I'd seen some paintings and photographs from Asia, China and Japan, I'd never assigned any importance to them, their culture being foreign and remote. I was not attracted to Eastern culture, the way many people were, following modern trends.

The feeling of disaster which accompanied me upon waking up disturbed me. At first I attributed it to the move to Palestine and the big changes in my environment. After all, Palestine was known as a place of unrest, due to the tension between Arabs and Jews; all the more so following the recent hostilities. But it didn't make any sense; I wasn't worried about the current political situation; and in my dream the disaster occurred very far away, nowhere near me.

Did the feeling of calamity perhaps hint at my personal life, the petering out of my love for Nathan? And who was that man in my dream? A man from such a different culture... was he a stranger or a partner? Perhaps it was Nathan in disguise? Was I dreaming about him, maybe concerned about the cooling down of my emotions for him? Was I experiencing guilt feelings? I had no answers, and even my intuition was of no help to me this time.

But maybe these sensations were a clue to a catastrophe that would take place far away, at home in Europe. I couldn't figure out the meaning of the dream, and unfortunately told no one about it. I kept it locked in the depths of my memory, and hoped that such dreams would never come true.

***

Letter to Zelda – 21 July, 1935

Zelda my beloved sister,

I miss you, and Karl, and of course Adam and mischievous little Zigush. We shall be meeting soon. *Ich bin oif mein veg aheym*, I'm on my way back home!

This letter is further to my previous letter, in which I wrote to you about my decision to return home. But please don't pass on the content of this letter to Mother. I can't bear to face her reaction should she read it.

One day my love for Nathan was gone – just evaporated, never to return.

I feel hemmed in. This is why I have decided to return to Chortkow after about two months here. I find Haifa too constricting. Not in the physical sense – Haifa is larger than Chortkow – but in terms of my way of life here. This constricting feeling is inside me. At first I accepted it willingly and was open to it. I was happy to fall in love with Nathan, and happy with the intensity of our clinging to each other. I was happy to be close to Junio and Malca, and even living close to Herman and Heidi suited me. But as the days went by, I began to feel locked up in a golden cage. Like a loving embrace that goes on and on until it becomes a grasp that you cannot escape from, leading to a feeling of suffocation.

The exotic atmosphere of foreign denizens, old neighborhoods and Middle-Eastern markets lost its charm, replaced by disgust with the dirt, the noise, and the foul smells. Only the amazing natural scenery, with its beautiful beaches, retained its magic.

Haifa is isolated, very far from Tel Aviv and Jerusalem in practical terms. The language difficulties and the awkward travel options to these cities make any trip complicated and hours-long, preventing me from following my usual independent and spontaneous habits, which are my normal way of life back home.

It is totally impossible here to get on a train at a moment's notice, and after an hour or two to be enjoying a concert, visiting a museum, watching a movie or a show at a respectable theater.

Very few of the people I know here in Haifa are my age. Junio and Malca are lovely and wonderful, and have been trying to make my life here as comfortable as possible.

But they and their friends seem like kids to me, and cannot replace the company I used to keep. I feel tired. I don't have the energy to move to Tel Aviv or Jerusalem on my own, to start looking for work and trying to create social ties from scratch. There is no demand for doctors here; the employment market is full of unemployed German physicians.

Also, I don't feel any spiritual elation. I guess that Zionism just isn't something for which I'm willing to make personal sacrifices.

Maybe I'm just the type who has difficulty adjusting to new people, places and cultures. I suppose that's what's creating a barrier between me and everything that's happening here, causing me to drop my plans and return home far sooner than planned.

I am finding it difficult to let Junio and Malca down. They hoped I'd stay with them, and that maybe you, too, would follow suit and join us. My breakup with Nathan also upset them. After all, Nathan and Junio became close friends, so naturally Junio and Malca were pleased to see us together.

Stark reality hit me hard when Nathan told me of his decision to return to Warsaw in line with his original plans, claiming he saw no professional future for himself in Palestine. That may have been a natural reaction to my becoming more distant. I can understand that. But still, I feel rejected and hurt. We said we'd keep in touch. He gave me his address in Warsaw and I gave him the phone number of my clinic in Chortkow. But the mere fact that he was sailing back two weeks before me says it all.

Zelda, please don't say *da vider comt dayn niggen*, "it's the same old story all over again"...

I know you're right, Zelda, but I can't change reality. True, I'm on a different continent, but I am the same Syma you've known all along who reached this continent, and I simply don't know how to change her.

I've decided to make a few stopovers on my way back – a few days in Athens and in Constantinople, then on the Polonia again to Constanta, and by train to Lwow. I feel that I owe myself a real European experience before returning home. I'd be delighted if you could join me for a few days. I'll be staying at the George Hotel in the center of town. I'll call you from Constanta before I leave for Lwow.

Du zalst nisht veinen iber mir adder mein goral, ich bin fein, "don't cry over me or over my fate". I'm fine. The past few months only proved to me what I've always known – I guess I just wasn't meant to be a wife and mother.

I must find the positive side of who I am, just the way I am, even if it's not "like everyone else". I look forward to being back with you all, back to my life in Chortkow, in my clinic. I am leaving Nathan in the past.

When we meet again, all I'll need is a big hug and your attention.

Dein mit liebe, yours with love,

Syma

***

On the Train – 18 November 1942

We spent the night in horrible loneliness. We were afraid to talk, to turn our heads, scratch our wounds, breathe. We sat close together, trying to find a bit of warmth. It was freezing out, the body ached to fall asleep but was afraid to lose control and collapse. Falling asleep and collapsing on the ground meant being shot in the head by the Ukrainian guards around us. So I sat with the others, in the square at the entrance to the Ternopol train station's main entrance, struggling to survive, to hang on to life. Dawn came slowly, as if reluctantly. First light was greyish, pale, then gradually the light became stronger, as if to illuminate a vision created by the devil: The transfer of the remnants, the remains of Chortkow's Jews, to an unknown future. Some said that over there, at the last stop, Jews were being exterminated; whereas others, like me, preferred to believe that we – physicians and other useful professionals – were being taken to the labor camps in the west in order to take care of the workers there. Other than us, there were no more Jews left in Chortkow. We were the last ones. We were picked up from Chortkow, Jagielnica, Buczacz, Husyatin, Borszczów, and all other towns in the district, as if trying to clean it up of Jews. We were the "privileged" ones, the "protected" ones. We believed that our occupations, which had protected us until today, would save us from a cruel fate. We knew about German cruelty, we saw how they murdered our families, neighbors, and friends. We saw how they took hundreds of people on a walk into the Black Forest, none of whom were ever seen again. Despite it all, we chose to believe in life, because there is always hope.

At six a.m. we were ordered to get up from the frozen ground and line up in threes. Gestapo men and Ukrainian guards surrounded us like a heavy belt and shoved us ahead as if we were cattle. After a short walk they made us run towards the station platform – that very same platform which I knew from a different life, the life of a young woman who had decided to become a doctor; from this platform I had left to study in Lwow.

They made us run towards the platform, hitting people indiscriminately with the stocks of their rifles, especially those who failed to keep up and those who dared to look around. And there, by the platform, stood the train; a freight train with perhaps forty or fifty freight cars. More groups of people kept arriving from different directions, men and women, some hanging on tightly to their children and some with babies in their arms. And then the loading began. The doors of the cars opened with a deafening noise, and the soldiers tossed inside torn bags of caustic lime which exploded on the floor of the cars, creating a white cloud which stung the eyes and clogged the throat. The Germans and Ukrainians stood on either side of the open doors, holding guns and whips with which they violently struck and beat the heads and faces of every person climbing into the freight car. I, too, took a strong beating, but for some reason did not feel any pain. At that moment I knew that I was no longer "protected". Women tried to stifle their crying, so as not to provoke additional beatings. The few children clung to their mothers and cried. Some threw up from distress. We pushed against one another, even stepping on the weaker ones, trying to avoid additional beatings and lashings. The freight-car was high above the ground and climbing into it was difficult. People were pushing and shoving, many got injured. But, despite the hell, order was maintained: exactly one hundred Jews in each car; no more, no less. Within about an hour the station was empty. The train doors were closed with a shrill squeak and locked with a thick metal chain, which I could just make out through the cracks between the boards of the car wall. I glanced around me. Men and women with work permits, professionals who until a moment ago believed they were immune, "safe", as we called ourselves, "the indispensable professionals". There were also a few young women, some of them with children, and middle-aged women, but no elderly. There were no elderly Jews in Chortkow. Their numbers had diminished day by day, until they were all gone.

The freight car was horribly, unimaginably packed. We were crammed, suffocating, sweating with fear, nauseous from the stench. The caustic lime made our eyes water and our breathing difficult. At that moment I understood that we were being led to the last stop of our life. To death. Death was already in the air. One could feel it. The train wasn't moving. The heat and stuffiness increased. There wasn't a single drop of water in the car and our thirst got worse, despite the freezing weather. It was impossible to sit down. All you could do was lean on the bodies closest to you, whether you wanted to or not. Surprisingly, no one got angry with anyone. A kind of indifference and apathy prevailed. People withdrew into themselves, groaned or wept quietly – men, women and children alike. Some prayed and asked for Heaven's help, help that surely would never come. Despair prevailed.

While we were still in the station, sanitation workers walked in carrying heavy firehoses, and began hosing down the platform, washing away within minutes any sign of what had just taken place there. I continued watching through the crack between the boards, and saw a train pulling into the station. It was the Thursday morning train from Czernowitz, which stops in Chortkow. It stopped on the other side of the platform, and the passengers began disembarking. They looked so calm and relaxed… some carrying suitcases, some talking to each other, some happy and laughing, as if living in a different world, a parallel universe, totally unaware of the hell we were in. Hell located just a few dozen yards from them. I stretched my neck and squinted, but did not recognize any of them.

At nine minutes past eight the train pulled out of the station. There was nothing to hang onto, but we were packed so close that I couldn't fall. The train accelerated fast, but for me time stood still. I knew, probably like everyone else around me, that this was most likely the last trip of my life. A trip to The End, an end I could not imagine.

In the sixteen months that had passed since the Germans entered Chortkow, our lives had turned into hell. People were debased, died of sickness and starvation or were tortured to death. I witnessed death every single day. Yet, I still had hope. Even though my prospect of survival was slim, many times I believed that the moment would come when I'd wake up from this nightmare and find myself in a different world.

Now I was trapped in a freight-train, fully conscious, and knew I was traveling towards my death.

The train stopped three times: at Kulikov, at Żółkiew, and at Rawa Ruska. I knew these stops well from my vacations in Lublin; they were meant for coordinating train traffic. And, indeed, within a few minutes, other trains passed by on the parallel tracks, some slowly, others at full speed. One train, coming from the west, had fancy Pullman sleeper cars, with German tourists inside. For a moment, it seemed like a scene from a different world: on one set of tracks people were being led to their death, while on parallel tracks tourists and businessmen were traveling in the comfort of first class.

The stench and rancid air in the car were unbearable. Many relieved themselves while standing in their spots, and the low sounds of weeping became louder. A few people around me lost consciousness and collapsed where they stood, yet remained supported by the pressure of the bodies around them. No one spoke, no one tried to soothe or encourage anyone else. Every person had withdrawn into himself, helpless, rocking with the movement of the train. Time stood still.

There was no way of escaping from the train. The freight car was relatively new, and it was impossible to move any of the wood boards along its sides. There was only one window, long and narrow, high in the wall opposite me. But it was so narrow that a person's head wouldn't have been able to fit through it, not to mention a body. Nonetheless, every once in a while we heard shots coming from the roof of the train. I thought it was the guards shooting at anyone who succeeded in breaking out of other cars, maybe older ones that did enable a desperate attempt at breaking free. Or who knows, maybe the guards were just having fun shooting at signposts along the way.

Worst of all was the thirst, which got worse with every minute. My throat was parched, my lips chapped, my skin and eyes burning from the caustic lime. What wouldn't I give for one sip of water. And I did have a lot to give: The Doxa wristwatch I wore, and gold ducats sewn into the lining of my coat, for emergencies. But there was no one who could be asked for water, nor any way of buying some, of course. When we stopped en route, the guards were quick to fire in the air to shoo away curious or good-hearted people who approached the train with bottles of water. That led me to conclude that the type of train I was on was a daily occurrence.

I did a quick calculation: There were a hundred people per car, about fifty cars per train, ergo, at this very minute some five thousand helpless people were being transported to an unknown location. Probably to their death.

***

Hope is the Enemy of Fear

The smell of death filled the air. A single thought kept going through my head, again and again, like the sound on a broken record: "Use the cyanide, use the cyanide, use the cyanide…" The pill was sewn into my coat lining along with three gold ducats. I'd given the second pill I had to my mother. And I already knew, by hearing on the grapevine in Chortkow, that my mother had used it, the moment the doors closed on that freight train into which she was thrust, about a month ago.

Hope is the enemy of fear, even when you are facing death. Hope is like that tiny ray of light which snuck through those cracks in the wall of the freight car, revealing that outside the sun is shining on a new day. That same hope overcame fear of the unknown, despite not having a chance in hell. In that split second, I surrendered to hope and did not take my fate into my own hands.

***

At the Belzec Station – 19 November, 1942

The train reached the Belzec station at noon. For a moment I thought that, once again, ordinary trains would be passing by and this nightmare of a trip would never end – but our trip was over. I couldn't believe that Belzec was our train's destination. Yes, there had been all sorts of rumors about what went on in camps around Belzec, but such rumors existed about every location to which Jews were transported.

We knew, for example, that the term "resettlement" included the possibility of work in forced-labor camps, working on roads and railways and clearing away snow in winter. And there were also rumors about camps where Jews were being murdered.

I didn't believe these rumors, not for a minute, because in my view they simply didn't make any sense. Why on earth would anyone transport Jews such a distance, when they could be exterminated "close to home". We all knew that in the Black Forest, for instance, Ukrainians had murdered thousands of Jews on orders from the Gestapo. Some had managed to crawl out of the ditches of the mass graves and returned to Chortkow, simply because there was nowhere else to escape to, and they described the horrors: First they were made to dig huge ditches, and as soon as they finished digging, they were shot and dumped into the ditch that they themselves had just dug. Many of our family, friends and acquaintances had been buried alive there.

Some Ukrainian railway workers talked about a terrible aktion, as those mass resettlements were called, that took place towards the end of August, some two and a half months ago, when thousands of Jews were transported to the Belzec "slaughter-house". One night they were cruelly forced onto a freight train in Chortkow, and none of them were ever heard from again. I did not believe this story. It didn't make any sense. I thought they were just trying to break our spirits. Because viciousness had no limits.

I didn't have much time to ruminate. The carriage door opened with a loud noise, letting in blinding light and freezing wind that smacked my face. I breathed in deeply, inhaling the fresh air, trying to rid myself of the foul smell that had stuck to my body.

Loud yelling in German sounded all around: "Los! Los! Los!" – "Go! Go! Go!" – Quick! Move it! Everyone understood immediately, we needed no interpretation. Get off the train, or more precisely, jump out. The cars were over three feet above the ground, and there was no platform, just a wide open space next to the train, surrounded by barbed wire fences. The next thing I heard was dogs barking, dozens of dogs, scary black German shepherds who welcomed us in their own language, as if saying, "Welcome to the gates of Hell".

Then came the shoving, the lashing and the beating, and, before I knew it, I found myself rolling on the muddy ground, wet from rain, or blood, or both. Dozens of SS men, along with skinny, bald-headed men who looked like prisoners, stormed the train, screaming and beating indiscriminately. The skinny men lashed us with their whips and the SS men hit us with the stocks of their rifles. Everyone hurried to get off, trying to avoid the beatings; people jumped off, fell down and rolled on the ground. Many were hurt, injured, broke arms and legs, and the ground was suffused with blood.

The only ones remaining in the cars were the dead. Those who had died during the journey but remained standing, crammed as they were between other bodies; or those who had fallen at our feet without our even noticing.

We were quick to comply with the instructions blaring out of the loudspeakers. Germans and their minions rushed at those who were sprawled on the ground, unable to get up – the exhausted elderly, the injured children, and those who had fainted – and threw them onto stretchers or simply grabbed them by their heels and dragged them over to a huge ditch at the end of the courtyard. My gaze was transfixed, as I saw a Gestapo man shoot them in the head then kick the bodies with his booted foot into the ditch, as if getting rid of some filthy obstacle.

My mind froze in horror. As I stood petrified, the announcer yelled at us to get into formation and, that murderer, who only a minute ago shot the victims in the head, walked over to the front row. Silence prevailed. Only then did I notice that there were no birds in Belzec. Complete silence. The weeping and moaning with pain stopped, everyone kept quiet, waiting for what would come. Then one sentence bellowed, loud and clear: "You are now going to the showers, then you'll be sent to work." Everyone breathed a sigh of relief. Some even gurgled happily. We thought we had been spared.

The men were being marched quietly, in perfect order, towards a nondescript building with a prominent sign, Baths & Inhalation Rooms. The women were roughly pushed, spurred by rifle beatings, towards a very large building, whereas the bald-headed young girls were sent along with the men. I hurried as fast as I could toward the large building, still believing that all would be well, and that after washing, we would undergo some kind of selection. In a place with so many employees, surely there is need for doctors, I thought naively; it made sense: the Germans, too, must be exposed to the many plagues rampant in the ghettos, and which we are probably bringing with us. Once more, for a moment, hope filled my heart.

When my turn came, I was forcefully shoved into the building. They let in eight women at a time. The room looked like a very basic hairdresser's place. We were told to get undressed so that the hair wouldn't get in the way or irritate our skin later on. Each woman was given a wooden stool. We were ordered to sit down. A bunch of barbers came over and within minutes our heads were completely shaven. I watched my hair fall down next to my naked legs. Only when we were instructed to get up and walk, naked, did I understand, for the first time, that my time was up. I didn't cry, I didn't feel sorry for myself. I guess in the past two years I'd had enough time to say my goodbyes, to my own life and to everyone in it: The first to leave was Ethel, my older sister, who traveled to America to be with her husband, only to be jilted. Next was Chaskel, my older brother, who left with his wife to go to South America. Then Junio, my kid brother, went to Palestine, followed by Malca, his wife. Then Father died. When Junio came back to Chortkow with Malca and Baby Ilana, to show her to the family, the war broke out, but they had managed to escape just in time. The first to be murdered by the Germans was Karl, my sister Zelda's husband. Then his son Adam, a gifted child, died from typhoid in my arms – I couldn't save him. Next, my sister Zelda and her son Zigush disappeared – I hope they managed to hide somewhere. About two months ago, Mother was taken to the trains. And last to escape was my beloved colleague and friend, Israel, a, who escaped with his family, leaving me all alone.

Naked from bald head to frozen toes, I was shoved out into the yard. The scene before me looked as if it were taken right out of Dante's Inferno.

Hundreds of women of all ages, naked, bald, their scalps a brilliant white, were standing in the freezing cold. Within seconds, the hope of staying alive was replaced by deep despair. It was clear to us all that our end was near. The silence made way to a whisper that gradually became louder until it became a howling sound, like that of an injured animal. Horrible wailing that became increasingly stronger. Some women clung to each other. Some lay down and tried to hold on to the ground. Some tried to pull out their non-existent hair and, when they couldn't find any hair to grasp, they beat their own heads until they bled. Many just stood there dumbly, a vacant look in their eyes. I must have looked like that. I don't know how long I stood there, while the stream of women being pushed into the yard didn't stop for a moment. Maybe I was standing there for only a few minutes – much less than it felt. My wristwatch had been taken from me, and I felt as if time stopped and life was drawing to an end extremely slowly.

I did not panic. I stood there frozen, looking around. To the right of the yard one couldn't see anything – just a fence and behind it a large, grey wall, through which I suppose the men went. To my left, through a narrow crack in the grey, wooden fence, I got a glimpse of the forest surrounding our location: tall, straight bare trees close together, creating a kind of silver crown, like a picture frame from a time gone by. Between the fence of the yard where I stood and the forest – which was about five hundred feet away – there were two long rows of what looked like huge flowerbeds without the flowers, beds of about three feet high, the likes of which I'd never seen. I couldn't understand what they were for; the soil looked freshly tilled. Next to them were dozens of strange-looking wheelbarrows. The sound of a band playing came from behind the fence. I thought I heard violins, flutes, and possibly an accordion. I think the musicians were all German. They played cheerful German tunes and Polish folk songs that were mixed with women's crying and wailing. At regular intervals of fifteen minutes or so an additional sound joined the band – something like the sound of a big truck approaching the wall. It added to the perfect Soundtrack of Hell. I felt detached from everything going on, as if I was merely a bystander, scanning the scene, watching all the small details, trying to take a mental picture of the last moments of my life, creating memories that would accompany me to Nowhere.

At the very far end, on the right-hand side of the courtyard, there was another grey building, towards which we were now pushed. The building was very low, as if it was an underground bunker and only its upper half was above ground. The building did not have any windows, only one large wooden door, with three steps leading down to it. Above the door was a large sign, similar to the one I saw earlier: Baths & Inhalation Rooms. As I was forcibly pushed towards the door, I saw by its side a lovely large flowerpot with purple, orange, yellow, pink and white flowers. A large splash of color, perhaps the last one I would ever see.

SS soldiers with bayonets in their hands jabbed our naked bodies indiscriminately. Bleeding, we escaped into the building, shoving and treading on each other. We crammed together through a low door into a large room without windows or an exit door. Its ceiling was very low and contributed to the stuffy, suffocating feeling. I was trembling with cold and fear. I felt that the end was near. We were crammed into one another in the packed room. I struggled to breathe the disgusting air – rancid, stinking of blood, sweat and fear. Suddenly the door was slammed shut. We were trapped, struggling for every breath.

At first, the women were all moaning and weeping quietly. Then the weeping turned into screams and shrieks of despair, in a jumble of languages. They screamed for their loved ones who were no more, and to a God that hasn't been listening for a long time now.

Once again I heard the sound of the truck engine, a loud sound that swallowed the screaming. This time the sound of the engine was very close, right near me, on the other side of the wall. The building trembled, or maybe it was I who trembled.

I imagined I felt hot air entering through the walls. Or maybe I wasn't imagining it.

I imagined I could smell the end. Or maybe I wasn't imagining it, because the end was here.

It came

***

Shaanxi Earthquake, China 1556

The Shaanxi earthquake is the deadliest earthquake recorded in human history.

Our knowledge of the Shaanxi Earthquake, also called the Huaxian Earthquake, comes from the custom of Chinese emperors to document important historical events and unusual natural phenomena. Writings from the court of Emperor Jiajing of the Ming Dynasty report the death toll to have been over eight hundred and thirty thousand.

According to local annals, the earthquake struck without warning on January 23, 1556. Its effects were felt over a large region encompassing ninety seven counties throughout the provinces of Shaanxi, Shanxi, Hunan, Jiangsu, Gansu, Hubei, Shandong, Habei, Henan, and Anhui. The earthquake resulted in unprecedented destruction and spanned over five hundred miles. In some areas more than half the population was killed. At that time, much of the population lived in artificial caves carved in soft silty stone, or clay houses. During the earthquake these collapsed, killing the inhabitants.

The scholar Qin Keda who lived through the earthquake describes it thus:

"In the winter of 1556 a catastrophe took place, caused by an earthquake in the Shaanxi and Shanxi Provinces. In our own Hua County there were many calamities. Mountains, hills, and rivers moved, and most roads were destroyed. In some places the ground rose suddenly, forming new hills and mountains. In other places the earth sank abruptly creating new valleys. In yet other places, a stream broke forth or the ground broke open creating new rivulets. Huts, public buildings, temples, and city walls all collapsed."

The powerful earthquake was felt strongly in the town of Nanshe in Guangdong. Residents reported odd behavior of animals, insects, and birds, and unusual changes in the level of waters in the canal in the hours prior to the event.

***

The Characters in the Story

Syma Finkelman (murdered in Belzec)	1899-1942
Nathan Hoffman	1895-1942
Yitzhak Finkelman (Syma's father)	1869-1933
Rivka Finkelman (Syma's mother, murdered in the Holocaust)	1870-1942
Junio, Shlomo Zvi Finkelman (Syma's brother, my father)	1908-1958
Melcha, Malca Finkelman, née Kramer (my mother)	1911-2013
Zelda Finkelman, Halstoch (Syma's sister)	1895-1955
Ethel Finkelman, Weitzman (Syma's sister)	1890-1958
Arnold Weitzman (Ethel's husband)	1889-1961
Fabiush, Philip Weitzman (Ethel's son)	1913-1991
Herman, Chaim Finkelman (a relative of Syma's)	1895-1963
Hedwig, Heidi Finkelman, née Wechsler (Herman's wife)	1898-1981
Yehuda Finkelman (Herman & Heidi's son)	1921-1963

About the Book

When writing my first book, Out of the Shoebox, I was surprised to find out that my aunt on my father's side, Dr. Syma Finkelman, arrived in Haifa in 1935 and stayed with my parents for a short while, around two months.

In June 2013, during my visit to the Belzec extermination camp in Poland, where Syma was murdered, I decided to tell her story.

Before sitting down to write the book, I spent two years doing thorough research, which continued throughout the writing process. Gradually, I learned about my parents'— Junio and Malca's – way of life in Haifa of the mid nineteen-thirties, and about the lives of their families in Poland during the years preceding World War II, in which many of my family members perished.

The facts and memories that I accumulated concerning Syma painted a picture of a tragic figure, who remained on her own until the end of her life. Syma had come to Palestine on a family visit, and also to look into the possibility of adapting to the country and maybe even immigrating there. The biggest tragedy of all was her unfortunate decision to go back home, to Chortkow.

Syma left Palestine following a personal crisis or as a result of becoming disappointed with the Zionist ideology, and thereby sealed her fate. Not long after, World War II broke out in Europe, and Syma died in an extermination camp that the Germans built on Polish ground.

The book describes two short periods in Syma's life: about two months in 1935, which she spent mostly in Haifa; and about forty eight hours in November of 1942, when she was forcefully taken to the Belzec extermination camp.

The chapters about the last forty-eight hours of Syma's life are based on my extensive research, including reading numerous testimonials describing both the trips in the "death train" that transferred Jews from Ternopol to Belzec and the operation of the extermination camp. All of which enabled me to learn what Syma went through, in factual terms, from the moment the train reached Belzec until her death; and let me imagine what she must have gone through emotionally.

The Belzec extermination camp began operating in March 1942 and was the first to carry out mass murder using Carbon Monoxide emitted by tank engines. The death-by-gas rooms were disguised as showers. The Nazis ended operations at Belzec in December 1942, after having killed some 600,000 Jews there. The entire camp was destroyed by the Germans during 1943, in an attempt to wipe out any trace of the extermination actions carried out there.

In an attempt to mislead the victims, a sophisticated, deceitful method was put in place, designed to give the victims hope until the last minute, hiding the fact that they were about to be murdered by poisonous gas. After the victims had been stripped naked and their hair shaved off, each victim received a small clay tag with a number imprinted on it, on a string for tying it on one's wrist like a bracelet, as if to enable each person to receive his/her clothes back after the so-called shower.

This camp was used solely for extermination by gas. According to documents I found, Syma reached Belzec on November 19, 1942, and apparently was killed that very day.

The earthquake in Shaanxi served as background for writing Syma's third dream.

***

Syma's registration form

Lwow National Medical University, Poland, 1918

July 11, 1924 – Document confirming Syma Finkelman's graduation from medical school and having qualified for a medical degree. The document is signed by the dean and the relevant professors. At the bottom of the document – Syma's first signature as a doctor.

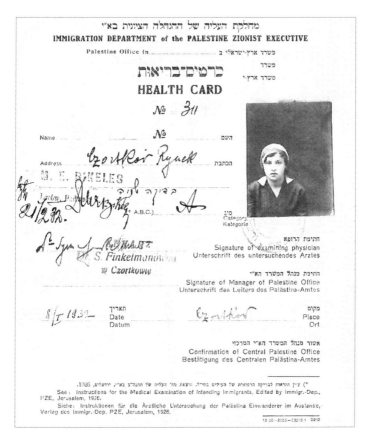

Health certificate issued by the Aliya (immigration) Dept. of the Jewish Agency, required for immigrating to Palestine. The examining physician – Dr. Syma Finkelman, Chortkow, January 8, 1932

Belzec Memorial Site, 2013

Below is the text I wrote on June 15, 2013, at the memorial site of the Belzec extermination camp, and which I read out loud that day, at the end of a ceremony commemorating ten years since the establishment of the museum and memorial site on the grounds of the camp. The ceremony was performed once the relevant documents were found in Ternopol – evidence that Syma was deported and transported by train to the Belzec extermination camp.

Syma, you left the Ternopol Center Platform on November 19th, 1942, and on that same winter day you arrived at Belzec. I assume that before the end of the day, your time had come, and you took your last breath.

Belzec was an extermination camp, not a concentration camp. It was a monstrous, well-oiled machine, that each day wiped thousands of Jews off the face of the earth, murdering them and destroying all memory of them, without keeping any records or documentation.

You and I are meeting today for the first time, seventy one years, seven months and six days since the day you arrived here. We meet on the same ground, the same place, under the same skies.

Syma, we did it! Your memory has not been erased. It will live on here, on this earth, in Belzec, and anywhere else in the world where people read about you. Your memory is safe and sound in the pages of the book which I wrote about our family, which is your new home. You have been granted eternal life; your memory lives on forever.

It is here, in Belzec, that I decided to write about you and tell your story. A story about a brave, ground-breaking woman, who in many ways was ahead of her time. A woman who was murdered, along with thousands from her city, on this very ground where I now stand.

May your memory be blessed forever.

***

Acknowledgements

It took two years of research before I sat down to actually write this book, and additional research continued throughout the writing process. I wish to thank all those who helped me find the relevant information, and especially Lia Halstuch who has become a vital partner in researching our family's history. Thanks also to Miri Gershoni, who has been researching and documenting the Chortkow community, for her immense help in collecting historical data.

Thanks first and foremost to my wife, Raya, for her support and invaluable insights that contributed to developing the characters in the book.

Thanks to Hanan, my business partner, who encouraged me to write, and who was always available for consultation and provided me with excellent feedback.

Yonatan, my son, and his wife Shani – thank you for your spot-on, much-appreciated comments.

Udi Ben Seadia – thank you for your insights, which assisted me in the process of writing and editing the story.

Thanks to Nina Davis, who translated the book into English and contributed much to its editing. Nina succeeded in being true to both my voice and language, and in helping the characters come to life.

Thanks to Yael Ornan and Keren Amram, form Notssa Publishing, for your comments, feedback and your excellent work, making this book available on Amazon.

Thanks to my friend Camilla Conlon for her thorough, conscientious proofreading of the English version of the book.

Last but not least, big thanks to my sister Ilana, for encouraging and urging me to write about our family, and for her part in enabling the publication of this book.

I am convinced that without the considerable help I received from these people, and others, the journey would not have taken place and this story would not have been told. For that I am eternally grateful.

***

Made in the USA
Columbia, SC
21 November 2024